Immigrants and Their International Money Flows

Immigrants and Their International Money Flows

Susan Pozo
Editor

2007

W.E. Upjohn Institute for Employment Research
Kalamazoo, Michigan

Library of Congress Cataloging-in-Publication Data

Immigrants and their international money flows / Susan Pozo, editor.
   p. cm.
   Includes bibliographical references and index.
   ISBN-13: 978-0-88099-299-2 (pbk. : alk. paper)
   ISBN-10: 0-88099-299-9 (pbk. : alk. paper)
   ISBN-13: 978-0-88099-325-8 (hardcover : alk. paper)
   ISBN-13: 0-88099-325-1 (hardcover : alk. paper)
   1. Emigration and immigration—Economic aspects. 2. Emigrant remittances. I. Pozo,
Susan.
   JV6217.I54 2007
   330.9172'4—dc22

                              2007011020

The facts presented in this study and the observations and viewpoints expressed are
the sole responsibility of the authors. They do not necessarily represent positions of
the W.E. Upjohn Institute for Employment Research.

Cover design by Alcorn Publication Design.
Index prepared by Diane Worden.
Printed in the United States of America.
Printed on recycled paper.

Dedicated to Ricardo, my son—and to Maria, my daughter, who for this year abroad has been an unwilling migrant.

Contents

Acknowledgments

As with any production, this one ran into a few unexpected turns of events and minor crises. But all of these were handled with calm and ease by the Upjohn Institute and others who partnered with me on this project. I would like to thank John S. Earle and Michael Ryan for being on my planning committee. And thanks again to Michael for helping out with many of the tasks that had to get done each time we hosted a speaker. Thank you to Kevin M. Hollenbeck and Richard Wyrwa for jump-starting the book production process. Many thanks go to Benjamin Jones for being such a super editor—for understanding what I really meant to say and for always finding a way to accommodate everyone's tastes. Thanks as well to Erika Jackson for typesetting the chapters, including the complicated formulae in one of them. Thanks also go to Chuck for always helping on both the home and the professional front. Finally, I would be remiss if I didn't thank the six contributing authors who came to campus for their willingness to share their insights on migration and remittances.

1
Migration and Remittances

Susan Pozo
Western Michigan University

In the mid-1940s, my father migrated to the United States from Uruguay. He met and married my mother (a Dominican immigrant) in New York City and never returned home again while his parents were living. His contacts with his family were infrequent, consisting only of a letter or two each year. In contrast to his separation from his family 60 years ago, my one-year sabbatical leave in Uruguay hardly feels so distant. Thanks to e-mail, Voice over Internet Protocol (VoIP), and digital photography, my parents don't miss a thing, and my husband and I and our 11-year-old daughter get to keep up with their daily lives, too. They know the details of each apartment we looked at before deciding on one, and we get the blow-by-blow on the balcony reconstruction going on at their condominium in Florida. Once a day or so we converse using Skype, an Internet telephony network, and if they are diligent about reading my husband's blog they will even get to see pictures of the chivitos (a typical Uruguayan sandwich) we ate for lunch today.

While it certainly is not the case that all migrants have the ability to travel with laptops, other aspects of the information technology revolution, including telephone cards with relatively inexpensive rates for calling internationally, are widely accessible all over the world. Internet cafes enable even those without regular telephone, electricity, or Internet service to have access to VoIP. In short, it is much easier for migrants to keep up with their families back home and for the families back home to keep up with the absent household member.

Remittances, the earnings that immigrant workers send back home in cash and in kind, are an important by-product of migration. The research community has only recently come to recognize the pervasiveness and growing magnitude of these international money flows. While the measurable growth in money transfers from emigrants to the families back home is likely due to a variety of factors, including better measurement techniques and an increase in the percentage of families with migrants, I strongly suspect that the ease with which migrants are now able to maintain contact with family back home is an important contributing factor to the observed growth and increased persistence of these flows. In effect, distance is not as great an obstacle for keeping in touch as it used to be. Those with jobs and earning power in their adopted homelands are better informed of the needs and desires of family back home. Remittances are less likely to taper off and are more likely to persist for a longer duration.

This book collects the papers from a yearlong lecture series held at Western Michigan University in Kalamazoo, Michigan, on the topic of international migration, with an emphasis on remittances.[1] An overriding theme that emerges from this collection is the need to appreciate the connection between international migration and remittances in order to fully understand either migration or remittances. Understanding what lies behind migration will often provide us with insights on remittances. But equally important is the need to fully understand the impacts of remittances, as this will provide us with insights about migration.

Some individuals migrate to better their economic standing, others to diversify the income streams of the family, and still others to reunite with family in the destination country. Families sometimes flee their home communities and countries on account of religious or political persecution. Some migrants leave home with the intention of permanently resettling in the foreign destination, while others migrate on a temporary basis—to study, to help a relative in need, to accumulate funds toward purchasing a large-ticket item. Regardless of the reasons for migrants leaving home, substantial inflows of remittances are common to many regions of the world experiencing emigration. While migration and some of its more obvious effects on the out-migration areas have been extensively studied, many aspects of these migratory flows are still poorly understood, including the return flow of money home. But as the contributors to this book point out, to get the full picture we need to understand the impact of remittances on the home communities and on migration in turn. A variety of reasons may explain the absence of research efforts in the area of international remittances, including misinformation about the true volume of flows and overly simplistic models of the motives of migrants who send money home. This book is intended to fill this void by offering the views of six migration scholars who came to the WMU campus to share their research in this area and to offer suggestions for additional efforts toward understanding this complex process.

The collection begins in Chapter 2 with a general overview of international migration by Robert E.B. Lucas, who notes that almost 10 percent of the population in richer countries is foreign-born, and that the majority of these foreigners originated in the developing and low-income world. Poor economic conditions at home are usually presumed to be the impetus for emigration, and a good deal of attention has been paid to that motive for migration. While understanding the connections between poverty and migration can further our understanding of population movements and their effect on the receiving country, Lucas notes that it is equally important to understand the economic impacts of migration for those areas experiencing out-migration.

Lucas suggests that while economic conditions may explain migration, migration in turn explains economic development back home. Disentangling the two can present a challenge for researchers. Nonetheless, Lucas discusses how emigration affects the well-being and economic behavior of those left behind. Emigration does so in several ways: through the remittances that are sent home, through changes in the labor supply of the remaining household members because of departing members, through exchange rate impacts, and through their effects on the human capital levels of the remaining population. Lucas makes clear that in some of these areas the research community is relatively well versed on those impacts, but that in other areas a consensus still has not emerged and we have much to learn concerning the results of out-migration.

Lucas's chapter brings to the forefront a fundamental point: whether governments acknowledge this or not, the immigration policies of the in-migration areas can and do significantly affect economic development in the low-income areas of the world. Debates on migration policy rarely consider the point that differing domestic policies on immigration will have differing consequences for migrant-sending areas of the world. Although there is little consideration given to this aspect of migration policy, economists should, at a minimum, provide policymakers with the facts and data that will present options for devising policies and programs that can lift low-income countries of the world. A better understanding of the consequences of migration policy should increase the odds that policy can be tailored to better benefit out-migration areas.

In this regard it is important that economists recognize the impacts of differing immigration policies and that they be in a position to inform policymakers of those results when policymakers craft immigration policies. In the book's third chapter, Oded Stark and C. Simon Fan provide additional backing for the notion that immigration policies in high-income areas might have unintended consequences for the out-migration areas.

Stark and Fan note that while it has long been recognized that unemployment in developing countries drives individuals to emigrate so they can join the labor force in the developed world, the notion that causality may also run in the other direction has not been adequately considered. As Stark and others have argued, the prospect of high earnings in the foreign destination may induce greater investments in human capital. In other words, rewards to education in the developed world may drive potential emigrants to spend more time in school and to acquire more skills, leading to "brain gain" in the developing economy. But what has not been adequately recognized is that those out-migration probabilities raise reservation wages (wage expectations) for those seeking to emigrate even while they wait for the opportunity to do so. Given that immigration restrictions in the developed world exist, an excess demand for visas results. Not everyone who wants to migrate gets to migrate, and, given the disparities in wage expectations and wage offers, "educated unemployment" persists.

Stark and Fan's model zeroes in on this educated unemployment phenomenon as an important channel by which the immigration policies of high-income countries affect economic conditions in lower-income areas of the world. Immigration policies that select more-educated immigrants can encourage unemployment in migrant-sending regions of the world, since such policies raise the supply of the better educated in areas with few opportunities for those skills. The authors lament that, to date, rigorous empirical analysis of the complicated interplay between migrant-sending and -receiving areas has been limited. It is important that we attempt to follow up on these relationships to better devise policies and to better understand the connection between brain drain and brain gain.

While the Lucas and the Stark and Fan chapters focus strictly on the impacts of migration and policy on the low-income world, in the book's fourth chapter Christopher Woodruff looks at the effects on both nations of traffic crossing back and forth over the border between the United States and Mexico, which he describes as the "largest unilateral flow of people (in one direction) and resources (in the other) in the world." Woodruff notes that 10 percent of the Mexican-born population resides in the United States—indisputably a massive movement of people across a national boundary. Equally important, and occurring in conjunction with this population movement, are the flows of monetary resources sent by Mexican immigrants in the United States back to their home communities and families.

Woodruff uses these significant bilateral flows to drive home an important point concerning the analysis of migration's impacts on out-migration regions: while it may be tempting to analyze the impacts of migration simply by comparing the outcomes in households with a migrant to those in households without a migrant, such a comparison is unlikely to provide us with reliable information on the effects of migration. This is because households that have experienced the migration of a family member are likely to differ fundamentally from households that have not experienced the migration of a family member. If we simply compare the two types of households, it will be unclear whether the differences observed are due to migration or to the underlying, unobserved, unmeasured characteristics that distinguish the two sets of households in the first place.

In reviewing the measurement issues, Woodruff considers three possible impacts of Mexican migration to the United States: 1) migration's impact on business investments in Mexico, 2) its impact on the health status of children, and 3) its impact on educational attainment.

He points out the pitfalls of using an empirical analysis that ignores the fact that migrant (and remittance-receiving) households are not randomly selected from the overall population. Instead, he directs us to appropriate strategies and techniques to compensate for the non-randomness so that we can properly measure the impacts of migration and remittances.

Using studies that employ appropriate measurement techniques, Woodruff concludes that while migration does not seem to induce new business formation, migration is responsible for substantial investments in microenterprises in Mexico. As for its effect on human capital, migration seems to promote educational investments in young children while decreasing these same investments in older children. Although child mortality rates are lower in families that have a migrant, researchers are discovering that migration has a negative effect on specific health investments that promote healthy outcomes. For example, doctor's visits and innoculations may be postponed because of monetary and other strains arising from the migration of a family member. Woodruff emphasizes the pains researchers must take to properly measure the separate impacts of migration and of remittances. He provides us with a number of methodologies that can be used to overcome these complex measurement problems.

The fifth chapter in this book concentrates on remittances from the United States to Latin America. Taking advantage of the wealth of information contained in the Latin American Migration Project (LAMP) survey, along with the more established Mexico-based survey, the Mexican Migration Project (MMP93), Catalina Amuedo-Dorantes provides us with a broad, comparative picture of the remittances that flow from the United States to six Latin American countries—Costa Rica, the Dominican Republic, Haiti, Nicaragua, Peru, and Mexico. In order to help the reader better understand these money flows, she discusses what the surveys reveal regarding who migrates and under what conditions they migrate to the United States. The surveys rely on information provided by return migrants. While there are significant differences by country in the proportion of return migrants who declare to have remitted during their last U.S. visit, she finds that on average 70 percent of the migrants claim to have remitted home during their last U.S. visit. They remitted an average of $300 a month, which was equivalent to 40 percent of their average monthly earnings.

The MMP93 and the LAMP also collect information on immigration status and on the use of smuggling services to undertake illegal immigration. Such information provides us with insights into the barriers that confront migrants as well as information on how these barriers are negotiated. This in turn hints at the likelihood of large monetary obligations incurred back home, which are likely to be reflected in the size of the remittances sent home: if would-be migrants need to contract for smuggling services, it is likely that they will have to remit large sums of money home to pay off those debts and obligations.

Of particular interest in the chapter by Amuedo-Dorantes is the cross-country comparison of the end uses of remittances. Considerable controversy exists regarding the types of expenditures that are undertaken with remittances. Are remittances used by the family remaining at home to finance consumption, or are they used to save and invest? The comparative nature of the surveys sheds light on this hotly debated issue.

In the sixth chapter, David J. McKenzie takes us to another region of the world, the South Pacific, where he examines another large migratory flow: the flow of Tongans to New Zealand, along with the return flow of New Zealand dollars to Tonga. One-third of Tongans have emigrated, and remittances account for 39 percent of Tonga's gross domestic product (GDP). The sheer magnitude of these flows makes the Tonga/New Zealand case one of interest.

McKenzie uses information from the Pacific Island–New Zealand Migration Survey (PINZMS), which queries respondents in detail on the channels used to remit. He supplements this with information he has collected concerning the costs of sending remittances from a number of high-immigration countries around the world to small island states. This permits him a unique perspective on the relative costs and constraints faced by Tongans remitting money home. In a nutshell, McKenzie finds that the relative costs for remitting in the case of Tongans residing in New Zealand are extremely high, and he offers suggestions for policy that may lead to a reduction in the costs of remitting and thereby increase the volume remitted.

McKenzie comes to several conclusions regarding the longer-term flow of remittances. He analyzes the relative expectations by remitters and remittees on the future flow of remittances. This information is crucial to the debate about the long-run impacts of migratory flows on out-migration areas. Some researchers have expressed concern that families in out-migration areas learn to depend on the regular monetary inflows from their family members abroad, letting their own human and physical capital depreciate. Such a concern would be especially critical if indeed recipients of remittances expected the monetary inflows to persist indefinitely. However, because of the nature of the survey, which matches recipients to senders, McKenzie is able to ascertain expectations regarding the future flows of remittances from the perspective of both agents. In the long run, both remitters and remittees expect remittances to decay with time. If remitters do get hooked on remittances, it is not because they falsely believe that the flows will persist indefinitely. The family at home seems to have reasonably realistic expectations about how long the flow of money from family members abroad will continue and to realize that over time the flow will diminish.

The book closes with a thought-provoking chapter by Leah K. VanWey that includes a typology of migration-remittance systems. The typology helps us categorize the three types of migration-remittances systems that are most common: 1) male household heads migrating in order to remit home with the purpose of supporting a wife and children, 2) children who migrate and send money back home to help parents, and 3) hometown associations of migrants that collectively remit to benefit the hometown community. Understanding these variations in migration-remittance systems enables us to identify the likely impacts of remittances in the home community, since they help distinguish remittances that are channeled into private consumption versus those that are channeled into investment and the public good.

Van Wey emphasizes that to truly understand the consequences that remittances have for migrant-sending communities, it is necessary to consider in greater detail the institutions that are in place in the home community, as these ultimately have an impact on remittances. Home community institutions can exert significant pressures on migrants to make financial contributions. Understanding the strengths and the pull of these institutions may give us a more thorough appreciation of the impacts of migration on economic development.

The chapters in this book all point to the multidimensional ties that exist between migrants in their adopted homes and the communities from which they originate. Wage disparities, often summarized as "push" and "pull" factors, certainly help explain migration, but the process is really much more complicated than that. The monetary flows that persist beyond the initial migration have significant and lasting impacts on migrant-sending regions of the world. These are important to account for if we are to truly understand migration and its long-run effects.

As the world's information and transportation infrastructure continues to grow, it is likely that emigrants will maintain even closer contacts with their home communities. The links between migrant-sending and migrant-receiving areas will likely get stronger. For this reason, now is an opportune time to help craft policies that will mold the contribution that immigrants can make both to their adopted and to their home communities.

Note

1. The series was the forty-second annual Werner Sichel Lecture-Seminar Series, hosted by the WMU Department of Economics and jointly sponsored by the W.E. Upjohn Institute for Employment Research and Western Michigan University during the academic year 2005–2006.

2

International Migration and Economic Development in Low-Income Countries

Lessons from Recent Data

Robert E.B. Lucas
Boston University

The links between international migration and economic development of the low-income countries have recently come to attract a good deal of attention: in 2005 the Global Commission on International Migration (2005) came out with its report, much of which focused on development implications for the low-income countries; the World Bank's *Global Economic Prospects 2006* was subtitled "Economic Implications of Remittances and Migration" (World Bank 2005); and in September 2006 the High-Level Dialogue on International Migration and Development took place at the General Assembly of the United Nations (UN).

Why is the migration-development nexus attracting so much attention now? Two key factors go a long way toward explaining the increased interest. First, international migration continues to grow. According to UN estimates, the stock of persons living in a country in which they were not born expanded by 14 percent from 1990 to 2000. The breakup of the former Soviet Union and of Yugoslavia accounted for some of this absolute increase, as internal migrants were suddenly now counted as international migrants. Most of the rest of the growth in migration simply reflects world population growth. In fact, migrants in 2000 remained close to their 1970 portion of world population, at about 3 percent. But what has really attracted attention is the absolute expansion in levels of migration to the higher-income countries. By 2000, almost 1 person in 10 in the developed regions was an international migrant. The foreign-born population of the United States grew by about 13 million during the 1990s, and the number of immigrant visas issued by the United States in that decade was similar to the number issued during the mass migrations from Europe in the first decades of the twentieth century. Indeed, immigration to both the United States and Canada has been on a long-term upward trend since the 1930s. But the national origins of those migrants are now quite different from those of earlier migrations to North America; European migrants have given way to new waves of Asian immigrants, and in the United States, Latin American migrants have also increased in importance. Meanwhile, Europe faced a flood of asylum seekers arriving during the 1990s. Some were fleeing from violence on Europe's edges, such as in the former Yugoslavia, but others came from much farther afield. Recognition rates of these asylum seekers were low to begin with and fell as more came. Yet the mass influx, coupled with the fact that the migrants' countries of origin had not been common sources of earlier migrants, provoked considerable attention among the European Union (EU) countries, which had never seen themselves as countries of immigration. Indeed, the EU member states still do not possess any coherent or mutually consistent immigration policies.

Besides the increasing numbers of international migrants, the second component that has attracted so much attention among researchers is the flow of remittances that is now being reported. The World Bank's *Global Economic Prospects 2006* reports that by 2004 remittances to the developing regions had grown to nearly US$160 billion (World Bank 2005). This was about 50 percent greater than all Official Development Assistance.

The link between, on the one hand, this growing interest among researchers, international agencies, and governments in international migration and, on the other, economic development in the lower-income countries of origin runs both ways: development at home shapes outward migration, while the process of migration simultaneously affects development in a number of ways. The next section of this chapter turns first to the former link: the effects of development on outward migration. Most of the rest of the chapter then addresses various aspects of the latter link: the effect of migration upon development at home.

THE CAUSES OF MIGRATION, AND THE EFFECTS OF DEVELOPMENT UPON MIGRATION PRESSURES

Migration outcomes (i.e., whether individuals are able to migrate) are a combination of the desire to emigrate and of constraints upon realizing those desires. Various forms of entry controls in the destination countries represent one obvious form of constraint. Yet these controls are far from being the only determinant of migration outcomes. The desire to migrate from a particular country shapes the application rate for legal entry. Moreover, no country has controls that are absolutely effective. Despite the militarization of the U.S. borders, the former Immigration and Naturalization Service (INS) estimated that the number of irregular migrants in the United States doubled between 1990 and 2000.[1] Estimates of the number of irregular migrants in the EU range as high as 10 million. Similarly, even such countries as Saudi Arabia and Japan, which have much tighter controls, have significant numbers of foreigners who have overstayed their visas.

Virtually all of the assembled evidence indicates that the gap in earnings opportunities for migrants between their home country and their overseas destination is a significant and important factor in driving migration flows. Thus, economic development at home—provided that job creation and a tighter labor market accompany this economic expansion—serves to diminish emigration pressures.

A counterargument has become widely accepted and is featured in a number of major reports on international migration, namely the concept of a migration hump. The idea is that at low income levels a rise in incomes serves to exacerbate emigration pressures, while at higher incomes a drop in income exacerbates emigration pressures. At least five hypotheses have been put forward as underlying the lower arm of a migration hump. They are enumerated as follows:

1) Rising incomes result in more rapid population growth, and the resultant population pressures are the root cause of additional emigration. Using this hypothesis, Hatton and Williamson (2002) posit that it was lagged population growth from about two decades earlier that drove the mass emigrations from Europe in the last century rather than rising incomes per se. On the other hand, very few countries are now in a phase in which

population growth is still increasing with development, so this hypothesis is of less relevance today.

2) Trade liberalization, undertaken in an attempt to accelerate development, can result in temporary job loss, and some of those displaced may emigrate.

3) A similar claim has been made with respect to the broader structural transformations (especially the shift from agriculture to industry) that generally accompany economic expansion. Note, however, that both of these latter arguments maintain that it is labor market slack that drives emigration pressures, which is consistent with the view that gaps in earning opportunities are a major causal factor in migration.

4) Rising incomes at home may ease credit constraints that previously prevented would-be migrants from financing costly migration abroad.

5) It has been suggested that the returns on remittances are higher in middle-income countries, making emigration and remittance to these states financially more attractive.

Although these hypotheses are all eminently reasonable, and although the notion of a migration hump is now fairly universally accepted, there appears to be little or no systematic evidence to support this pattern; rather, evidence supports the contrary, that at lower income levels a rise in incomes serves to relieve emigration pressures, while at higher incomes a drop in income relieves emigration pressures.

This is illustrated in Figure 2.1, which shows net annual migration per thousand of population from 1995 to 2000 for 164 countries. (Negative outcomes reflect net out-migration.) The horizontal axis displays the natural logarithm of gross domestic product (GDP) per capita, measured in purchasing power parity U.S. dollar prices. The two superimposed lines are a simple linear regression line and a spline regression. The simple linear regression line indicates a significant positive association: lower-income countries tend to have higher rates of net emigration, and higher-income countries exhibit more net immigration. More importantly, the spline variant clearly shows that the lowest-income countries do not have very low rates of net out-migration, contrary to what a migration hump would suggest.

Figure 2.1 Relationship of Gross Domestic Product to Net Migration for 164 Countries, 1995–2000

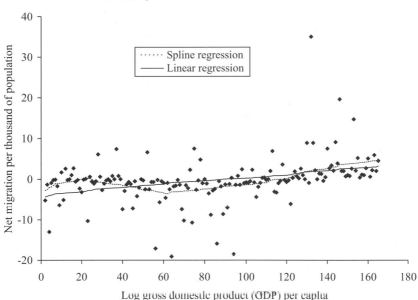

SOURCE: United Nations Development Programme (2002); United Nations Population Division (2003).

Although most existing studies support the notion that emigration diminishes as income levels and earning opportunities at home improve, there is considerable noise around this association, as is clear in Figure 2.1. Development is by no means the only factor affecting migration outcomes: geography is important, too. This is brought out in Figure 2.2, which shows the percentages of each of the non-OECD countries' populations present in the OECD member states as of 2000.[2] First, it is apparent that there is a great deal of movement among the OECD member countries themselves, very often to neighboring members. Beyond that, the high emigrations from the Caribbean and Central America to the United States are evident, as are the large migrations from the Maghreb, Eastern Europe, and parts of the Middle East to the EU. The countries with high migrations to the OECD nations from further away tend to be countries that have spawned large numbers of refugees, such

Figure 2.2 Non-OECD Country Populations Present in OECD Member States, 2000 (%)

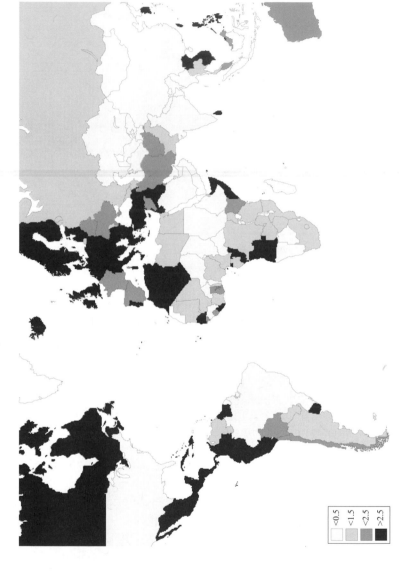

<0.5
<1.5
<2.5
>2.5

SOURCE: Docquier and Marfouk (2005).

as Somalia, Angola, and parts of Indochina, though there are exceptions (such as the Philippines).

In fact, geography seems to be even more important than income levels and earning opportunities in shaping the migration of low-skilled workers. Figure 2.3 is similar to Figure 2.2 but shows only the percentages from each country of the adult populations in the OECD with nine years of education or less. Two aspects of the data in Figure 2.3 are of particular note. First, some of the OECD member countries are themselves major sources of low-skilled migrants in the OECD. Not surprisingly, large numbers of low-skilled workers are present from Mexico and Turkey, both of which are OECD members. But other countries, such as those of southern Europe, are also key sources of low-skilled workers within the OECD. In fact, 32 percent of the low-skilled migrants in OECD countries are from OECD members other than Mexico and Turkey. The second aspect to note is that very few low-skilled workers gain access to OECD countries from countries that are distant from the OECD regions.

Yet this does not mean that countries whose populations are largely unskilled do not have significant out migration. Indeed, as the map in Figure 2.4 shows, a number of countries in low-income regions exhibit fairly high rates of net out-migration even though their stock of migrants in the OECD is not particularly large. This is a reflection of the importance of south-south migrations, which often form the dominant option for low-skilled workers from the low-income countries. For instance, Figure 2.4 shows quite high rates of net emigration from Indonesia, Burkina Faso, and Kazakhstan, though emigration rates from these countries to the OECD regions are relatively low. Meanwhile, some of the better-off countries within the developing regions, such as Malaysia and Gabon, underwent significant net immigration.

A major example of south-south movement has been the mass migrations to the Persian Gulf from South and Southeast Asia as well as from some of the lower-income countries in the Middle East. Many observers thought this process was coming to an end with the decline in oil prices in the early 1980s, but in fact there was a resurgence during the 1990s, involving a wider spectrum of source countries. But other, less well-known movements are important too: from Indonesia to Malaysia; from large parts of sub-Saharan Africa to South Africa, to Gabon, and to

Figure 2.3 Non-OECD Country Adult Populations Present in OECD Member States with Nine Years of Education or Less, 2000 (%)

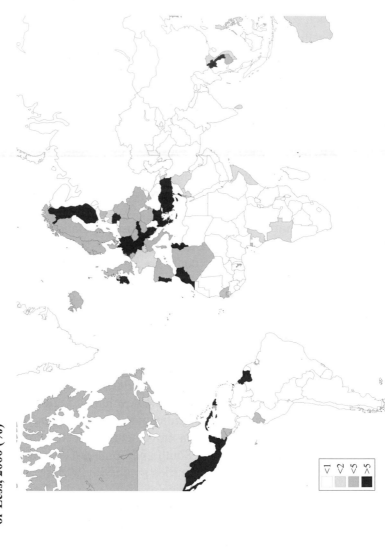

SOURCE: Docquier and Marfouk (2005).

Figure 2.4 Rates of Net Out-Migration, 1995–2000 (%)

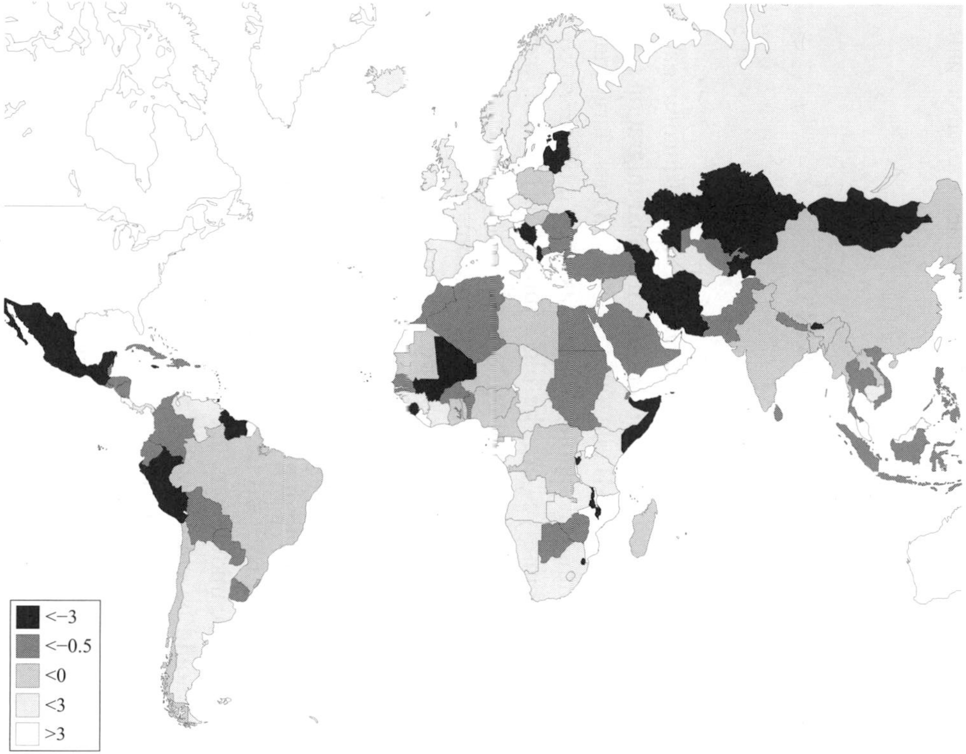

Legend:
<–3
<–0.5
<0
<3
>3

SOURCE: United Nations Development Programme (2002); United Nations Population Division (2003).

other higher-income countries within the region; from Burma to Thailand; from Bangladesh to India; and many more.

Economic development, geography, the incidence of violence, and many other factors help to shape these complex patterns of migration. But what are the effects of the migrations upon economic development at the migrants' place of origin? What underlies the other half of the migration-development link?

THE EFFECTS OF MIGRATION UPON ECONOMIC DEVELOPMENT

Simulations suggest that there are huge global income gains to be had even from a small expansion in international migration (Walmsley and Winters 2003; World Bank 2005). The key to these large gains is the increases in earnings available to migrants upon moving. Accordingly, the migrants themselves are the big winners. In practice, part of the gains to migrants are siphoned off by various middlemen. In particular, both legal and irregular migrations have become increasingly commercialized, so that recruiters and smugglers now command a significant fraction of the rents to be had from migration. Indeed, the limited available evidence suggests that the lower the income of the migrant's country of origin, the higher this rent extraction becomes (Lucas 2005, pp. 275–288). Because the migrants have almost nothing to begin with, the large gains to be realized in these lower-income contexts give greater leverage to the middlemen.

It should be emphasized that the net gains to the migrants themselves are a form of economic development for the nationals of the country of origin, even if these income gains are not drawn from domestic production. The effect of migration upon the incomes of those left at home is an important one, but the answer to the question of what kind of an effect it has is generally ambiguous. Although such elements as tighter labor markets at home and the gains resulting from remittances sent by departed migrants may relieve the economic situation at home, the potential for effects such as brain drain to act in the opposite direction is very real. One should not expect a uniform answer to whether emigration helps or hurts those left behind.

Remittances

Transfers of remittances from migrants may be divided into two types: those that pass through formal sector intermediaries, versus those that are transmitted through myriad money dealers in the informal banking network. The latter generally prove cheaper and faster. The official data on remittances, as reported by the International Monetary Fund (IMF), refer largely to formal remittances, though even these data are subject to substantial measurement error. Little systematic information exists on informal transfers, though for some low-income countries informal receipts appear to be relatively large.

The effect of remittances upon people left at home has been the subject of considerable controversy and some confusion. Other things being equal, receipt of such transfers must raise the standard of living. But whether the combined effect of departure of the migrants and receipt of their remittances raises standards of living for those remaining at home is far less clear. Moreover, whether remittances are spent in such a way as to accelerate the rate of growth of home-country production is also unclear. Indeed, it is common for researchers to complain that too little investment occurs out of remittances and even for officials to direct policy to encourage such investments. Such efforts are largely misdirected. Officials of the home country may well feel that too little is being invested in their nation's economy, yet why the recipients of remittances should be singled out to undertake the additional investments remains unjustified. Remittances are a private form of income and should be subject to the same rights and privileges as other forms of private income. To be sure, artificial barriers to private investments should be dismantled, but this is true no matter whether these investments are financed out of remittances or otherwise.

The extent to which remittances serve to alleviate poverty in the home area depends upon the propensity of poor people to migrate, and, once they have migrated, upon their propensity to remit. In addition, the indirect effects on poverty alleviation are influenced by the multiplier effects of remittance spending and by any job creation that occurs as a result of additional investment coming from the inflow of remittances. Researchers have devoted most of their attention to remittances' direct effect on alleviating poverty. The extent to which current remittances alleviate poverty through this direct effect seems to be sensitive to how one defines the poverty level of families—whether by asset possession or current earnings—and to whether earnings are defined at the level they were at before or after the migrant left. Nonetheless there appears to be relatively uniform agreement that remittance inflows indeed do alleviate poverty, and in some instances this effect is estimated to be large.[3] The poor do migrate, even internationally, though perhaps more so internally. The poor also do remit. However, in a number of regions the very poorest are left out of this cycle of international migration and remittance receipt.

There is also growing evidence that remittances serve as a key element to ensure smoother consumption patterns for families in low-income countries. Given the vagaries of farming, many families in developing regions see their incomes fluctuate substantially between good and bad years. Add to this such risks as the family's main wage-earner getting ill or a natural disaster occurring, and prospects can be quite uncertain. A plausible response to these threats is to have some family members migrate to places where they will be unlikely to meet with the same misfortune. Then, if disaster does strike back home, the migrant can support those family members in trouble by remitting. Research has brought to light several examples of situations where helping to stem a crisis appears to be reflected in observed remittance patterns.[4]

Azam and Gubert (2002) note that one can generally expect moral hazard responses to the insurance provided by remittances. Specifically, families that receive remittances may well react by reducing their labor effort at home. This argument is supported by findings in the Kayes area in western Mali, where household survey data indicate that although families of migrants have greater agricultural assets, their crop production is actually lower than that of nonmigrant families. Moreover, Azam and Gubert's results illustrate that this pattern is not simply a result of a smaller number of family workers available at home following the departure of migrants, nor a reflection of families with lower productivity tending to have members that migrate more. Certainly these findings are consistent with a growing body of literature demonstrating that, upon receipt of remittances, families enjoy part of the rise in living standards in the form of additional leisure.[5]

A second impact of remittances upon the labor market at home may also be noted. To the extent that remittances provide a sufficient amount of foreign exchange to support the exchange rate, they also make exporting more difficult. This effect, which is sometimes referred to as the "Dutch disease" effect of remittances, can serve to limit employment creation in the export sector, potentially leading to greater pressures to emigrate.[6]

Labor Market Impacts at Home

Apart from the effects of remittances through moral hazard in labor supply and through the exchange rate upon employment creation, the departure of migrant workers can readily affect the labor markets at home more directly. The withdrawal of migrants typically will either put pressure on home country wages to rise or will at least shorten the queue for jobs, depending upon whether or not the market has a labor surplus. More generally, migration's overall impact on the home country's labor market will also depend upon the extent of internal migration induced to replace departing workers and upon the skill mix of those migrating. A key element is whether the skills possessed by emigrants are complements or substitutes for the skills of those who remain at home. For example, the departure of highly skilled workers could raise the earnings of their direct competitors at home yet lower the demand for less-skilled workers who would have worked alongside those departing migrants in ancillary positions (Davies and Wooton 1992).

Rather surprisingly, although the issue of immigration's impacts on the labor market has been the subject of extensive research, the issue of emigration's impacts upon labor markets in countries of origin remains largely neglected. Certainly no generalizations appear possible at this juncture.[7] Nonetheless, how the home country's labor market performs for highly skilled persons proves central to determining how much damage is done by the brain drain.

Brain Drain, Brain Gain, and Brain Overhang

Figure 2.5 shows the percentage of each country's tertiary educated population residing abroad in an OECD country in 2000.[8] Although this percentage omits emigration of the highly skilled to non-OECD countries, on which no systematic data exist, Figure 2.5 nonetheless offers a good picture of the incidence of the brain drain flowing from developing to industrialized regions. Particularly high rates of brain drain

Figure 2.5 Tertiary Educated Population of a Country Residing Abroad in an OECD Country, 2000 (%)

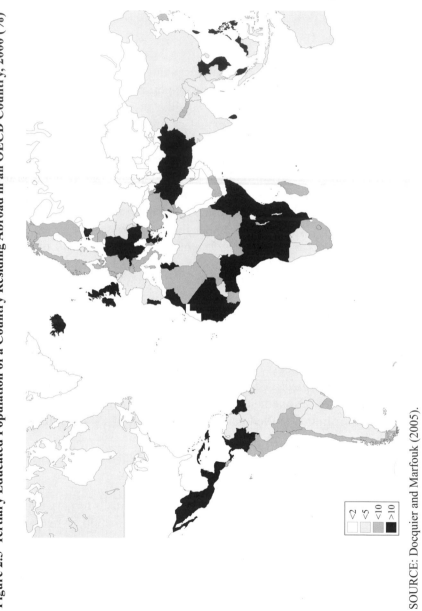

<2
<5
<10
>10

SOURCE: Docquier and Marfouk (2005).

are observed from Central America and the Caribbean, Eastern Europe, parts of the Middle East and Indochina, and across almost the whole of Africa.

North America, and the United States in particular, is the principal destination for these highly skilled migrants. European firms have only recently joined the race to attract the highly skilled, and Europe's foreign population is dominated by lower-skilled workers. Even the exodus of highly skilled professionals from Eastern Europe and the Commonwealth of Independent States (consisting of 11 former Soviet republics) occurred mostly to the United States during the 1990s, not to neighboring Western Europe.

Do the low-income countries lose from this departure of their most talented and highly educated? Chief among the potential sources of harm commonly cited are the following three types of loss: 1) the loss of economic growth, since such growth generally correlates with the presence of educated persons; 2) the loss of external benefits (such as better governance) that come with the presence of highly skilled compatriots; and 3) the loss of public funds invested in the highly skilled, as well as the loss of funds that would be taxed from their incomes at home. Each of these losses is controversial. Although the presence of highly skilled people is correlated with faster growth and with various beneficial outcomes such as the aforementioned better governance, whether this presence is the causal factor remains in dispute. Moreover, if there are any benefits, the question of whether the highly educated themselves reap the lion's share of these benefits in the form of higher incomes remains untested. And whether the highly educated make a net contribution to the fiscal balance is also contentious, since public spending on the highly educated and their families is often greater. On the other hand, the loss of public funds invested in the highly educated is much clearer in countries that heavily subsidize higher education of even the children of elite families.

A separate but closely related aspect of these potential losses is countries' inability to deliver key social services, such as health care and education, without trained personnel. The mass recruiting of health care workers from Africa has attracted particular criticism in the face of the HIV/AIDS epidemic there, not to mention malaria and other diseases that ravage the continent. Yet it is not clear that the emigration of doctors and nurses from Africa is the main constraint on the ability of African states to offer better health care (Clemens 2006). Indeed, across the spectrum of professions and in all developing regions, the inefficient use and allocation of the highly skilled classes raise serious doubts about the real costs imposed by their departure—a feature that might be called "brain overhang."

But many observers go even further, claiming that emigration of the highly skilled can confer benefits on their country of origin through the activities of a professional diaspora, which has become known as "brain gain." The best documented of these arguments is that a diaspora may have a beneficial effect on promoting trade with the home country; it does this by its members improving the flow of information between the home and the destination countries and by their ability to enforce contracts (Rauch 2001). For example, it seems the presence of Indian IT professionals in this country was critical to expanding India's software exports to the United States (Saxenian 2004). Other routes that can lead to beneficial effects and are commonly cited, but far less well documented, involve the transfer of technology and the promotion of direct investments in the home country.

However, the aspect of brain gain that has perhaps attracted the most attention recently is the inducement to expand education at home. The idea is that the emigration opportunity afforded by higher education induces greater college enrollments, and that only a fraction of those thus attracted to continue their education will actually manage to leave the country. If the stock of the highly educated population left at home thus expands, domestic production may then be improved (Mountford 1997; Stark and Wang 2002). Some observers may express reservations about this: the expansion of home education is hardly costless, and the freshly attracted students may be less competent, for instance (Schiff 2005). But perhaps more importantly, the evidence across countries does not seem to support this hypothesis, though certainly in some specific countries (such as the Philippines) enrollment in higher education indeed appears to be quite sensitive to overseas opportunities (Lucas 2005, Box 4.1).

SUMMING UP: POLICIES AND PROSPECTS

The effects of emigration upon economic development for those remaining at home are mixed. The effects are typically more poverty-alleviating, and possibly more positive for development in general, in cases where migrants are drawn from the lower-skilled parts of the labor force. It also tends to be true that the effects upon incomes of those remaining at home are more positive when the return rate (or at least the intended return rate) of migrants is higher. For instance, the massive remittances resulting from migration to the Persian Gulf are largely a reflection of the enforced family separation and the temporary nature of these movements.

Virtually none of the high-income countries really think of their migration policies as part of a more coherent development policy for the lower-income regions. Indeed, the competition among firms in the high-income countries to attract the best and the brightest from the developing regions is heating up: an ever-increasing number of industrialized countries are actively recruiting foreign students, often with the express intent of keeping the most successful. Meanwhile, almost all of the high-income countries have in place massive agricultural subsidies and protect low-skilled manufacturing activities. Both agriculture and manufacturing employ irregular migrants from the developing regions.

However, the low-skilled workers thus brought to the OECD countries tend to come from nearby nations that are not among the lowest-income countries. In fact, the force of geography is such that the propensity of countries to send their low-skilled workers to the OECD regions rises significantly with the income level of the originating country.

Temporary migrations of low-skilled workers probably have the biggest impact on poverty reduction in the developing regions of any type of migration. Most high-income countries seem to prefer temporary migrants to permanent ones and have expanded several of their temporary migration schemes. Yet such schemes face a fundamental dilemma: attempts to integrate migrants, to promote their rights, and to enable family reunification all tend to discourage return migration. On the other hand, the family and social costs can be high from government approaches to temporary migration that prevent legal family accompaniment.

What we probably need to seek are better ways of managing such temporary migrations. Certainly a number of steps seem eminently feasible to encourage greater return rates. Extending Mode 4 of the General Agreement on Trade in Services (GATS) to encompass low-skilled services may be one such critical step.[9] Establishing transferability of pension schemes to the home country is another. The use of intermediary contracting of projects appears to be particularly effective in ensuring that migrants return home, though such schemes need closer regulation to prevent abuse of the contract workers.[10] Ironically, irregular migrants are discouraged from returning home when the prospect of recrossing the border becomes more formidable.

In practice, only a few developing countries actually have very high emigration rates to the industrialized nations. Distance deters migration, both internally and internationally (Lucas 2001). Social networks help to amplify migration streams, once initiated. The combined effect is that remote countries, and remote villages within countries, are left out of the migration process. Where migration is never initiated, the community becomes increasingly isolated from a growing migration flow, both internally and globally, and pockets of poverty remain there. Yet south-south migrations often present migration opportunities of shorter distance, and consequently in today's setting they may represent the most important vehicles of poverty relief through migration from the lowest-income countries.

This picture could change. Communications, transportation, and commercialization of movement are all increasing. Moreover, the demographic map will shift dramatically over the coming decades. Most migrants are young adults, typically ages 15–30. By far the fastest growing populations in this age range are in sub-Saharan Africa (Lucas 2006). The world may well witness a rapid Africanization of international migration in the next half century—not just within the African continent, which is the dominant pattern at present, but out of Africa too.

Notes

1. On March 1, 2003, the INS was relocated from the Department of Justice to the Department of Homeland Security and split into three agencies: the Bureau of Citizenship and Immigration Services, the Bureau of Customs and Border Pro-

tection, and the Bureau of Immigration and Customs Enforcement. "Irregular" migrants are undocumented or illegal migrants.

2. The OECD, or Organisation for Economic Co-operation and Development, is composed of 30 market democracies and is dedicated to helping governments tackle the economic, social, and governance challenges of a globalized economy.

3. See, for example, Tingsabadh (1989) on Thailand, Gustafsson and Makonnen (1993) on migration of Lesotho's mine workers to South Africa, Lachaud (1999) on Burkina Faso, Adams and Page (2003a) on North Africa, and Adams (2005) on Guatemala, plus Adams and Page (2003b) for more global evidence.

4. See Lucas and Stark (1985) on Botswana, Hoddinott (1992, 1994) on western Kenya, Brown (1997) on Pacific Island migrants, Schrieder and Knerr (2000) on Cameroon, Gubert (2002) on the Kayes areas of western Mali, and Quartey and Blankson (2004) on Ghana.

5. See Funkhouser (1992) on Nicaragua, Rodriguez and Tiongson (2001) and Yang (2004) on the Philippines, and Amuedo-Dorantes and Pozo (2006) on Mexico.

6. For an early discussion of this point, see Quibria (1997). *The Economist* coined the term "Dutch disease" in 1977 to describe the manufacturing sector's decline in the Netherlands after natural gas was discovered in the North Sea in the 1960s. Deindustrialization followed because the discovery of this natural resource raised the value of the Dutch guilder, making manufactured goods less competitive with those of other nations, thus increasing imports and decreasing exports.

7. For a review, see Lucas (2005, pp. 85–102).

8. See also Dumont and Lemaître (2004).

9. In GATS, a treaty of the World Trade Organization, Mode 4 deals with the international movement of people in the process of delivering international trade in services.

10. "Contracting" here refers to a firm taking on a project abroad and bringing workers from abroad to execute this project.

References

Adams, Richard H., Jr. 2005. "Remittances, Poverty and Investment in Guatemala." In *International Migration, Remittances, and the Brain Drain*, Maurice E. Schiff and Çaglar Özden, eds. Washington, DC: World Bank, pp. 53–80.

Adams, Richard H., Jr., and John Page. 2003a. "Poverty, Inequality and Growth in Selected Middle East and North Africa Countries, 1980–2000." *World Development* 31(12): 2027–2048.

———. 2003b. "International Migration, Remittances and Poverty in Developing Countries." Policy Research Working Paper No. 3179. Washington, DC: World Bank.

Amuedo-Dorantes, Catalina, and Susan Pozo. 2006. "Migrátion, Remittances and Male and Female Employment Patterns." *American Economic Review Papers and Proceedings* 96(2): 222–226.

Azam, Jean-Paul, and Flore Gubert. 2002. "Those in Kayes: The Impact of Remittances on Their Recipients in Africa." DIAL Working Paper No. DT/2002/11. Paris: Développement, Institutions and Analyses de Long terme.

Brown, Richard P.C. 1997. "Estimating Remittance Functions for Pacific Island Migrants." *World Development* 25(4): 613–626.

Clemens, Michael. 2006. "Do No Harm: Is the Emigration of Health Professionals Bad for Africa?" Paper presented at the Myron Weiner Seminar Series on International Migration, Massachusetts Institute of Technology, held in Cambridge, MA, February 28.

Davies, James B., and Ian Wooton. 1992. "Income Inequality and International Migration." *Economic Journal* 102(413): 789–802.

Docquier, Frédéric, and Abdeslam Marfouk. 2005. "Measuring the International Mobility of Skilled Workers (1990–2000)—Release 1.1." Washington, DC: World Bank. Photocopy.

Dumont, Jean-Christophe, and Georges Lemaître. 2004. "Counting Immigrants and Expatriates in OECD Countries: A New Perspective." OECD Social, Employment, and Migration Working Paper No. 25. Paris: OECD Directorate for Employment Labour and Social Affairs.

Funkhouser, Edward. 1992. "Migration from Nicaragua: Some Recent Evidence." *World Development* 20(8): 1209–1218.

Global Commission on International Migration (GCIM). 2005. *Migration in an Interconnected World: New Directions for Action.* Report of the Global Commission on International Migration. Geneva: GCIM.

Gubert, Flore. 2002. "Do Migrants Insure Those Who Stay Behind? Evidence from the Kayes Area (Western Mali)." *Oxford Development Studies* 30(3): 267–287.

Gustafsson, Bjorn, and Negatu Makonnen. 1993. "Poverty and Remittances in Lesotho." *Journal of African Economies* 2(1): 49–73.

Hatton, Timothy J., and Jeffrey G. Williamson. 2002. "What Fundamentals Drive World Migration?" NBER Working Paper No. 9159. Presented at the WIDER Conference on Poverty, International Migration and Asylum, held in Helsinki, Finland, September 27–28.

Hoddinott, John. 1992. "Rotten Kids or Manipulative Parents: Are Children Old Age Security in Western Kenya?" *Economic Development and Cultural Change* 40(3): 545–565.

———. 1994. "A Model of Migration and Remittances Applied to Western Kenya." *Oxford Economic Papers* 46(3): 459–476.

Lachaud, Jean-Pierre. 1999. "Envoi de fonds, inégalité et pauvreté au Burkina Faso." Documents de travail 40. Bordeaux: Centre d'Economie du Développement de l'Université Montesquieu—Bordeaux IV.

Lucas, Robert E.B. 2001. "The Effects of Proximity and Transportation on Developing Country Population Migrations." *Journal of Economic Geography* 1(3): 323–339.

———. 2005. *International Migration and Economic Development: Lessons from Low-Income Countries*. Northampton, MA: Edward Elgar.

———. 2006. "Migration and Economic Development in Africa: A Review of Evidence." *Journal of African Economies* 15(2): 337–395.

Lucas, Robert E.B., and Oded Stark. 1985. "Motivations to Remit: Evidence from Botswana." *Journal of Political Economy* 93(5): 901–918.

Mountford, Andrew. 1997. "Can a Brain Drain Be Good for Growth in the Source Economy?" *Journal of Development Economics* 53(2): 287–303.

Quartey, Peter, and Theresa Blankson. 2004. "Do Migrant Remittances Minimize the Impact of Macro-volatility on the Poor in Ghana?" Final Report Submitted to the Global Development Network. Washington, DC: International Monetary Fund. http://www.imf.org/external/np/res/seminars/2005/macro/pdf/quarte.pdf (accessed October 23, 2006).

Quibria, M.G. 1997. "Migration, Remittances and Trade: With Special Reference to Asian Developing Economies." In *International Trade and Migration in the APEC Region*, Peter J. Lloyd and Lynne Williams, eds. Oxford: Oxford University Press, pp. 84–98.

Rauch, James E. 2001. "Business and Social Networks in International Trade." *Journal of Economic Literature* 39(4): 1177–1203.

Rodriguez, Edgard R., and Erwin R. Tiongson. 2001. "Temporary Migration Overseas and Household Labor Supply: Evidence from Urban Philippines." *International Migration Review* 35(3): 708–725.

Saxenian, AnnaLee. 2004. "The Bangalore Boom: From Brain Drain to Brain Circulation." In *IT Experience in India: Bridging the Digital Divide*, Kenneth Keniston and Deepak Kumar, eds. Bangalore: National Institute of Advanced Studies, pp. 169–181.

Schiff, Maurice. 2005. "Brain Gain: Claims about Its Size and Impact on Welfare and Growth Are Greatly Exaggerated." In *International Migration, Remittances, and the Brain Drain*, Çaglar Özden and Maurice Schiff, eds. Washington DC: World Bank, pp. 201–225.

Schrieder, Gertrud, and Beatrice Knerr. 2000. "Labour Migration as a Social Security Mechanism for Smallholder Households in Sub-Saharan Africa: The Case of Cameroon." *Oxford Development Studies* 28(2): 223–236.

Stark, Oded, and Yong Wang. 2002. "Inducing Human Capital Formation: Migration as a Substitute for Subsidies." *Journal of Public Economics* 86(1): 29–46.

Tingsabadh, Charit. 1989. "Maximizing Development Benefits from Labour Migration: Thailand." In *To the Gulf and Back: Studies on the Economic Impact of Asian Labour Migration*, Rashid Amjad, ed. New Delhi: ILO–ARTEP, pp. 303–342.

United Nations Development Programme. 2002. *Human Development Report 2002: Deepening Democracy in a Fragmented World*. New York: Oxford University Press.

United Nations Population Division. 2003. *World Population Prospects: The 2002 Revision. Highlights*. ESA/P/WP.180. New York: UN Population Division, Department of Economics and Social Affairs.

Walmsley, Terrie Louise, and L. Alan Winters. 2003. "Relaxing the Restrictions on the Temporary Movements of Natural Persons: A Simulation Analysis." Centre for Economic Policy Research Discussion Paper No. 3719. London: Centre for Economic Policy Research.

World Bank. 2005. *Global Economic Prospects 2006: Economic Implications of Remittances and Migration*. Washington, DC: World Bank.

Yang, Dean. 2004. "International Migration, Human Capital, and Entrepreneurship: Evidence from Philippine Migrants' Exchange Rate Shocks." Gerald R. Ford School of Public Policy Working Paper No. 02–011. Ann Arbor, MI: University of Michigan.

3

The Effect of International Migration on Educated Unemployment

Oded Stark
Universities of Klagenfurt, Bonn, and Vienna;
Warsaw University;
ESCE Economic and Social Research Center, Cologne and Eisenstadt

C. Simon Fan
Lingnan University

There are two salient features of many writings on human capital in developing countries. First, a fraction of the educated workforce migrates to developed countries. Since educated workers are one of the scarcest resources in developing countries, it has been argued that the migration of educated workers is a "brain drain" for the developing countries.[1] Second, in a number of developing countries, a large fraction of the educated workforce is unemployed. For example, in their influential development economics textbook, *Economics of Development*, Gillis et al. (1996) allude to the Sri Lankan experience as a striking example, noting that half of the country's new university graduates were unemployed in the 1970s.[2] The phenomenon of educated unemployment in those developing countries contrasts sharply with the pattern of unemployment in developed countries. In the latter, the unemployment rate and educational attainment are strongly negatively correlated (Ashenfelter and Ham 1979).

However, while there has been extensive research on the brain drain,[3] the issue of "educated unemployment" has attracted little attention in the economics literature, despite references to its importance in development economics textbooks. A notable exception is an article by Bhagwati and Hamada (1974). In a fixed-wage framework, Bhagwati and Hamada argue that a high foreign wage can increase the fixed wage rate of the educated in the home country by affecting people's psychology and that, in turn, the higher fixed wage increases unemployment.[4] However, since educated unemployment is not a serious problem in all of the developing countries, Bhagwati and Hamada could not explain why a high foreign wage affects the psychology of people in some countries but not in others.

This chapter provides an alternative model of educated unemployment. In the model developed here, educated unemployment is caused by the prospect of international migration, that is, by the possibility of a brain drain. In a simple job-search framework we show that an individual's reservation wage in the labor market of the home country increases with the probability of working abroad. Consequently, workers who fail to line up employment abroad are less likely to immediately immerse themselves in work in their home country. Instead, they enter unemployment in order to engage in a repeated attempt to secure foreign employment. Thus, we provide a new explanation for the phenomenon of educated unemployment observed in developing countries. Our theoretical analysis provides a basis and a rationale for rigorous empirical tests of this important phenomenon—tests that, to the best of our knowledge, are absent in the received literature. Moreover, our main argument that international migration and educated unemployment are closely linked seems to be consistent with considerable anecdotal evidence and policy-related research.[5]

We integrate the educated unemployment–international migration perspective with the recent literature on the "beneficial brain drain,"[6] which contends that compared to a closed economy, an economy open to migration differs not only in the opportunities that workers face but also in the structure of the incentives that they confront: higher prospective returns to human capital in a foreign country impinge favorably on human capital formation decisions at home. The analysis contained in this chapter shows that a developing country may end up with more educated workers despite the brain drain and educated unemployment. In other words, the average level of human capital in the country may well be higher under migration than in the absence of migration. This higher level can play a positive role in determining long-run future output growth, the present-day gloom of educated unemployment notwithstanding.

The next two sections of this chapter, "Migration and educated unemployment" and "The choice of acquiring higher education," set up the basic analytical framework and present a model of educated unemployment. The fourth section presents an analysis demonstrating that the prospect of international migration can lead to a "brain gain" despite brain drain and the possibility of being unemployed after acquiring a higher level of education. The final section offers conclusions and complementary reflections.

MIGRATION AND EDUCATED UNEMPLOYMENT

Consider a world that consists of two countries: home, H, and foreign, F. Country H is developing and is poorer than country F, which is developed. Because of a policy of selective migration by F, only educated individuals (say, university graduates) of H have a chance of working in, hence migrating to, F.

In this section we analyze the behavior of the home country's educated individuals. In the next section we incorporate into the model the cost of education and we analyze the decision to acquire education.

For our purposes, we assume that everyone in H is educated. The decision-making process of an educated individual is illustrated by Figure 3.1. According to this model, an educated individual makes decisions in (at most) three stages:[7]

The first stage. When an individual graduates from a university in H, the individual participates in a lottery draw that results in probable work in F. If the individual obtains a winning ticket, his income will be w^f. The probability of being selected to work in F is p.

The second stage. (Note that there is no second stage for individuals who win the draw.) An individual who graduates and fails to secure work in F faces the following choices: to work or to wait for another draw. Waiting for another draw frees up time to search for a job in F. Alternatively, if the individual were to work, little time (and energy) would be available for preparing applications and, in addition, the indi-

Figure 3.1 Stages in the Decision-Making Process of an Educated Individual

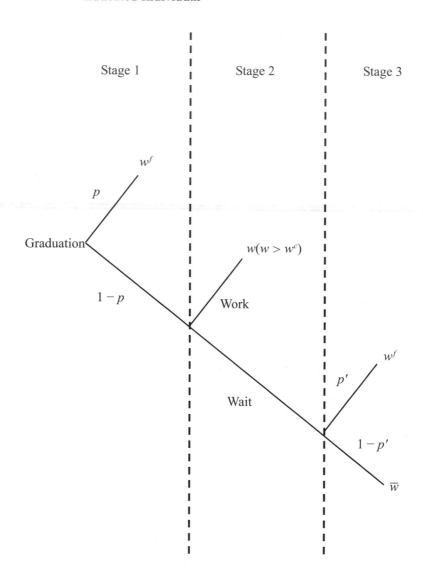

vidual's academic qualifications could depreciate, thereby lowering the probability of being picked up for work in F.[8]

The assumption that individuals choose unemployment while waiting for another draw of going abroad is particularly consistent with the job-search theory. In fact, the assumption that the probability of finding a (new) job is higher when an individual does not hold a job, but instead concentrates on searching for a job, is at the heart of the literature on job search and the natural rate of unemployment (Mortensen 1986; Acemoglu and Shimer 1999; Rogerson, Shimer, and Wright 2005). The rationale underlying this assumption is that searching for a job requires time and effort. The received job-search theory refers to domestic markets. It is reasonable to assume that finding a job in a foreign labor market requires even more time and effort.[9]

For simplicity's sake, we assume that if the individual works, he cannot participate in any additional draw, so his probability of ending up working in F is zero. If the individual does not work and awaits another draw, his chances of going abroad are p'.

The third stage. (Note that the third stage only applies to those who waited for another draw in the second stage.) If an individual wins this draw, he will go abroad. Otherwise, he will work at home, receiving the home country's mean wage rate.

The job offers in the second and third stage follow an independently identical distribution. The cumulative distribution function of the wage offer, $\tilde{w}$, is $F(w)$. We assume that $F(w)$ is differentiable. We also assume that

$$\tilde{w} \in [w^l, w^h]$$

and that the density function,

$$\frac{dF(w)}{dw} \equiv F'(w),$$

is strictly positive in its domain, that is,

$$F'(w) > 0 \quad \forall w \in [w^l, w^h].$$

The expected income of the (risk-neutral) individuals in the third stage is

(3.1) $(1 - p')\bar{w} + p'w^f$,

where $\bar{w}$ is the mean wage in H, namely

$$\bar{w} = \int_{w^f}^{w^h} w \, dF(w) \, .$$

In the second stage, if the individual receives a wage offer w at H, he will accept it if and only if

(3.2) $w > \dfrac{1}{1 + r} [(1 - p')\bar{w} + p'w^f]$,

where r is the individual's discount rate.

We define

(3.3) $w^c \equiv \dfrac{1}{1 + r} [(1 - p')\bar{w} + p'w^f] \, .$

In this case, the individual will accept the wage offer at H if and only if $w > w^c$. Thus, w^c is the individual's reservation wage at H.

Further simplifying, we assume that

(3.4) $w^f \geq \dfrac{1}{1 + r} \bar{w}$;

educated unemployment will not exist in the absence of an additional possibility of migration (that is, when $p' = 0$).[10]

Then, the fraction of the educated who are unemployed[11] is

(3.5) $u \equiv P(\tilde{w} \leq w^c) = F(w^c) \, .$

Clearly,

(3.6) $\dfrac{du}{dp'} = \dfrac{du}{dw^c} \dfrac{dw^c}{dp'}$

$$= F' \dfrac{w^f - \bar{w}}{1 + r} \, .$$

Note that the assumption that F is developed and H is developing naturally implies that $w^f > \bar{w}$. Since $F' > 0$,

(3.7) $\dfrac{du}{dp'} > 0$.

In addition, we note that

$$w^c \equiv \frac{1}{1+r}[\bar{w} + p'(w^f - \bar{w})]$$

and that

(3.8) $\dfrac{du}{d(w^f - \bar{w})} = F'\dfrac{p'}{1+r} > 0$.

In summary, we have the following proposition:

Proposition 1: *1) The unemployment rate of university graduates in a developing country will increase as the probability of migration rises. 2) The unemployment rate of university graduates in a developing country will increase as the wage gap between the developed country and the developing country increases.*

Proposition 1 implies that in a developing country, educated unemployment is caused by the prospect of international migration, that is, by the possibility of a brain drain. The greater the probability of being selected for work in the foreign country and the greater the wage gap between the foreign country and the developing country, the more serious the educated unemployment problem. The intuition underlying the proposition is straightforward. From Equation (3.3) we can see that w^c increases with p' and with w^f, and that it decreases with $\bar{w}$, which means that the individual's reservation wage in the home labor market increases with the probability of working abroad and with the international wage gap. Consequently, the unemployment rate will increase as the reservation wage rises.

Moreover, we have assumed for the sake of simplicity that only educated individuals (say, university graduates) of the home country have a chance of working in, hence migrating to, the foreign country. If we modify this assumption slightly, so that a better-educated individual in a developing country faces a higher probability of working abroad, then by similar logic to Proposition 1, we will obtain the result that the unemployment rate is higher for individuals with higher education.

THE CHOICE OF ACQUIRING HIGHER EDUCATION

The benefit that education without migration confers is simply H's mean wage rate of educated workers, $\bar{w}$. When migration is a possibility, the expected payoff from the three stages described in the preceding section is

$$
(3.9) \quad V \equiv pw^f + (1+p)\left\{ \int_{w^c}^{w^h} wdF(w) + F(w^c)\left[\frac{p'w^f +(1-p')\bar{w}}{1+r}\right]\right\}
$$

$$
= pw^f + (1-p)\left[\int_{w^c}^{w^h} wF'(w)dw + F(w^c)w^c\right].
$$

Clearly,

$$
(3.10) \quad \frac{dV}{dw^f} = p + (1-p)\left[-F'(w^c)w^c + F'(w^c)w^c + F(w^c)\right]\frac{dw^c}{dw^f}
$$

$$
= p + (1-p)F(w^c)\frac{p'}{1+r} > 0 .
$$

Let us assume that

$$
(3.11) \quad p' = p(1+\alpha) ,
$$

where α is a fixed parameter. To ensure that $0 < p' < 1$, we assume that

$$
-1 < \alpha < \frac{1}{p} - 1 .
$$

Then,

$$
(3.12) \quad
\begin{aligned}
\frac{dV}{dp} &= w^f - \left[\int_{w^c}^{w^h} wdF(w) + F(w^c)w^c\right] \\
&\quad + (1-p)\left[-F'(w^c)w^c + F'(w^c)w^c + F(w^c)\right]\frac{(w^f - \bar{w})(1+\alpha)}{1+r} \\
&= w^f - \left[\int_{w^c}^{w^h} wdF(w) + F(w^c)w^c\right] + (1-p)F(w^c)\frac{(w^f - \bar{w})(1+\alpha)}{1+r} .
\end{aligned}
$$

We further assume that

$$
(3.13) \quad w^f > w^h .
$$

To rule out the unreasonable possibility that all the educated are unemployed, we assume that

(3.14) $w^c < w^h$.

It follows that

$$\int_{w^c}^{w^h} w\, dF(w) + F(w^c)w^c$$

$$\leq \int_{w^c}^{w^h} w^h\, dF(w) + F(w^c)w^h$$

$$= w^h \int_{w^c}^{w^h} dF(w) + F(w^c)w^h$$

$$= w^h[F(w^h) - F(w^c)] + F(w^c)w^h$$

$$= w^h .$$

Therefore,

(3.15) $w^f > \left[\int_{w^c}^{w^h} w\, dF(w) + F(w^c)w^c \right]$,

and it then follows from Equation (3.12) that

(3.16) $\dfrac{dV}{dp} > 0$,

that is, the benefit of acquiring a university education in H increases as the probability of migration rises.

We next incorporate the cost of acquiring education. Our idea is that individuals differ in their abilities and familial background, hence in their cost of acquiring education. We normalize the size of the (premigration) population of H to be Lebesgue measure 1. Suppose that an individual's cost of obtaining education, c, follows the uniform distribution $\tilde{c} \in [0, \Omega]$.

We assume that the (lifetime) income of an uneducated individual is constant, and we denote it by Φ. Then, recalling the assumption that only individuals with university degrees have any chance of migrating, we see that an individual will choose to acquire a university education if and only if

(3.17) $V - c \geq \Phi$.

Let us define

(3.18) $c^* = V - \Phi$.

It follows that an individual will obtain a university education if and only if his cost of education maintains

$c \leq c^*$.

Since $\tilde{c}$ follows a uniform distribution and the population size of the economy is of Lebesgue measure 1, both the proportion and the number of educated individuals are given by

(3.19) $\dfrac{c^*}{\Omega}$.

From Equation (3.18) we get

(3.20) $\dfrac{d(c^*/\Omega)}{dp} = \dfrac{1}{\Omega}\dfrac{dV}{dp} > 0$,

where the inequality sign in Equation (3.20) follows from Equation (3.16). We thus have the following proposition:

Proposition 2: *The number of individuals undertaking university education will increase as the probability of migration rises.*
This proposition implies that while the prospect of migration causes the unemployment rate of educated individuals in the home country to increase (Equation [3.7]), it also induces more individuals to acquire education (Equation [3.20]). The end result may be an increase in the number of unemployed university graduates. Thus, Propositions 1 and 2 provide an explanation for the phenomenon of educated unemployment by linking it to migration.

A BRAIN DRAIN VERSUS A BRAIN GAIN

In this section, akin to Stark, Helmenstein, and Prskawetz (1997, 1998), we seek to examine whether the prospect of migration can result in a larger number of educated individuals in the home country. Since in our model only educated individuals have a positive probability of migration, it follows that if the prospect of migration results in a larger number of educated individuals in the home country, then it will *a fortiori* result in a higher fraction of educated individuals in the home country.

The following proposition shows that the brain gain caused by the prospect of migration may be larger than the loss from the brain drain.

Proposition 3: *There exists a positive level of* p *at which the number of university graduates remaining in the developing country is higher than the number of university graduates in the developing country when* p = 0, *for any given* α, *if* $w^f > (3 + \alpha)\overline{w}$.

Proof: We first note that c^* is a function of V and hence of p, so we define it as

$$(3.21) \quad c^* \equiv c(p) .$$

Then, under the migration prospect, the number of university graduates remaining in the developing country is

$$(3.22) \quad \frac{c(p)}{\Omega} - \left[p\frac{c(p)}{\Omega} + (1 - p)\,p'\frac{c(p)}{\Omega}F(w^c) \right]$$

$$= c(p)\left[(1 - p)(1 - p(1 + \alpha)F(w^c))\right] /\Omega .$$

Let us define

$$\frac{K(p)}{\Omega} = \frac{c(p)(1 - p)[1 - p(1 + \alpha)F(w^c)]}{\Omega} - \frac{c(0)}{\Omega} ,$$

so that $\dfrac{K(p)}{\Omega}$ is the difference between the number of educated individuals in the home country when $p > 0$, and the number of educated individuals in the home country when $p = 0$.

Since

$$K(p) \equiv c(p)(1 - p)[1 - p(1 + \alpha)F(w^c)] - c(0),$$

we know that

$$K(0) = 0$$

and that

$$K'(p) = c'(p)(1 - p)\left[1 - p(1 + \alpha)F(w^c)\right]$$

$$-\left\{1 - p(1 + \alpha)F(w^c) + (1 - p)(1 + \alpha)\left[F(w^c) + pF'(w^c)\frac{(w^f - \overline{w})(1 + \alpha)}{1 + r}\right]\right\}c(p).$$

We seek to show that $K'(0) > 0$ which, by the continuity of $K(p)$, would imply that $K(p) > K(0)$ in the small (positive) neighborhood of $p = 0$. Note that

$$K'(0) = c'(0) - [1 + (1 + \alpha)F(w^c)]c(0).$$

When $p = 0$, we know from the assumptions in Equations (3.4) and (3.11) that educated unemployment will not exist in the absence of an additional possibility of migration, which implies that $w^c = w^l$. Then, from the last line of Equation (3.12) and from the consideration that $F(w^l) = 0$, we get

$$\frac{dV}{dp}\Big|_{p=0} = w^f - \left[\int_{w^c}^{w^h} w dF(w) + F(w^c)w^c\right] + (1 - p)F(w^c)\frac{(w^f - \overline{w})(1 + \alpha)}{1 + r}$$

$$= w^f - \left[\int_{w^l}^{w^h} w dF(w) + F(w^l)w^l\right] + (1 - p)F(w^l)\frac{(w^f - \overline{w})(1 + \alpha)}{1 + r}$$

(3.23)　　　$= w^f - \overline{w}.$

Also, from the equality in Equation (3.20), we know that

$$\frac{dc^*}{dp} = \frac{dc(p)}{dp} = \frac{dV}{dp}.$$

Therefore,

$$\frac{dc(p)}{dp}\bigg|_{p=0} = c'(0) = \frac{dV}{dp}\bigg|_{p=0} = w^f - \overline{w} \ .$$

When $p = 0$, $V = \overline{w}$. Hence, from (3.18) and the definition $c* = c(p)$, we get

(3.24) $c(0) = V - \Phi$
$\qquad\ \ = \overline{w} - \Phi \ .$

Thus, $K'(0) > 0$ if and only if

(3.25) $w^f - \overline{w} - [1 + (1 + \alpha)F(w^c)](\overline{w} - \Phi) > 0 \ .$

Since

$\qquad 1 + (1 + \alpha)F(w^c) < 2 + \alpha \ ,$

Equation (3.25) will be satisfied if

$\qquad w^f - \overline{w} - (2 + \alpha)(\overline{w} - \Phi) > 0 \ ,$

that is, if

(3.26) $w^f > (3 + \alpha)\overline{w} - (2 + \alpha)\Phi \ .$

And since $\Phi > 0$, it follows that when $w^f > (3 + \alpha)\overline{w}$, Equation (3.26) will be satisfied, in which case we will have the result that

$\qquad K'(0) > 0.$

Hence, by the continuity of $K(p)$, it must be that $K(p) > K(0)$ in the small (positive) neighborhood of $p = 0$. ∎
Proposition 3 shows that a developing country may end up with more university graduates despite the brain drain of university graduates. If we consider that there is a reduction of the population in the wake of migration, the proposition also implies that the developing

country may end up with a higher fraction of educated individuals, despite the brain drain of university graduates.

Combining Propositions 1 and 3 yields the following corollary:

Corollary 1: *A positive level of educated unemployment in a developing country coexists with a larger number of university graduates in the country than the number of university graduates in the country under no educated unemployment if* $w^f > (3 + \alpha)\overline{w}$.

Since there are fewer individuals in the country under feasible migration, and since there are more educated individuals in the country under feasible migration, it must follow that the average level of human capital in the country is higher under migration than in the absence of migration. This higher level can play a critical role in determining long-run output growth, an issue to which we will turn in a future work.

CONCLUSION

Since the late 1960s, the development economics literature has pointed to a stark connection between migration and unemployment: workers change their location, but not their productive attributes, in response to an expected wage at destination that is higher than their wage at origin, only to end up unemployed (Todaro 1969). We propose a different connection between migration and unemployment wherein workers move into unemployment at origin in response to an expected wage at destination, and workers improve their productive attributes. While the flight of human capital and the unemployment of human capital occupied the center stage of development economics at about the same time (the 1970s), analysts and policymakers did not make a causal connection between the two phenomena except for noting that unemployment induced a desire to migrate. Our analysis considers a link: in a simple job-search framework, we show that an individual's reservation wage in the home labor market increases with the probability of working abroad. Thus, our model implies that such unemployment would be smaller in the absence of the migration possibility. Furthermore, we integrate our model into the recent literature of beneficial brain drain. The analysis shows that a developing country may end up with more educated individuals despite the brain drain and educated unemployment. Our theoretical analysis provides a basis and a rationale for rigorous empirical tests of the link between international migration and educated unemployment, which are absent in the received literature. Such empirical endeavors will constitute an interesting topic for future research.

Notes

We are grateful to Gordon Hanson and to an anonymous referee for helpful advice, enlightening comments, and constructive suggestions. Financial support from the Humboldt Foundation, the Sohmen Foundation, and the International Centre for the Study of East Asian Development is gratefully acknowledged.

1. For a systematic review of this argument see Bhagwati and Wilson (1989).
2. Also, Mathew (1997) reports that in urban Kerala, India, in 1983, the unemployment rate of university graduates was 11.34 percent for males and 25.69 percent for females, which is much higher than the unemployment rate of those who had no education (3.52 percent for males and 1.52 percent for females) and than the unemployment rate of those who had up to primary education (6.73 percent for males and 8.43 percent for females). More recently, Bourdarbat (2004) shows that in 2000, the unemployment rate of university graduates in Morocco was about four times that of individuals who had acquired less than six years of schooling.
3. The topic of the brain drain is also regularly taken up in the informed press (see the short overview in Stark [2004]).
4. For example, Bhagwati and Hamada (1974, p. 20) state, "The presence of international income-inequality implies that, for the educated elite which is better informed about the developed world, and more integrated therewith regarding the notions of a 'good life' and related values, the salary levels demanded and fixed by the elite groups tend to reflect the salary levels of comparable groups in the more developed countries."
5. For example, see King (1987) and Tullao (1982).
6. For example, see Stark, Helmenstein, and Prskawetz (1997, 1998); Mountford (1997); and Stark and Wang (2002).
7. We assume that relative to the duration of the individual's working life, the duration of the three stages is short.
8. Schaafsma and Sweetman (2001) show that "working experience in the source country yields virtually no return in the host country."
9. Information on the employment status of migrants at home in developing countries prior to migration is scanty. Rudimentary studies suggest that on several occasions, nearly half of the migrants from India were unemployed prior to migration (Srivastava and Sasikumar 2003). Additional empirical work on the em-

ployment status of individuals prior to their international migration would be of considerable interest.

10. Although this assumption is not necessary, resorting to it highlights the notion that educated unemployment is caused by the prospect of migration.

11. Note that in the current model, to facilitate our concentrating on essentials, unemployment applies only to stage 2 of the individuals' decision-making processes.

References

Acemoglu, Daron, and Robert Shimer. 1999. "Efficient Unemployment Insurance." *Journal of Political Economy* 107(5): 893–928.

Ashenfelter, Orley, and John Ham. 1979. "Education, Unemployment, and Earnings." *Journal of Political Economy* 87(5): S99–S116.

Bhagwati, Jagdish N., and Koichi Hamada. 1974. "The Brain Drain, International Integration of Markets for Professionals and Unemployment: A Theoretical Analysis." *Journal of Development Economics* 1(1): 19–42.

Bhagwati, Jagdish, and John D. Wilson. 1989. *Income Taxation and International Mobility*. Cambridge, MA: MIT Press.

Bourdarbat, Brahim. 2004. "Employment Sector Choice in a Developing Labour Market." Photocopy. University of British Columbia, Vancouver, BC.

Gillis, Malcolm, Dwight H. Perkins, Michael Roemer, and Donald R. Snodgrass. 1996. *Economics of Development*. 4th ed. New York: W.W. Norton.

King, A.M. 1987. "Philippines." In *Migration of Talent: Causes and Consequences of Brain Drain: Three Studies from Asia*, Yogesh Atal and Luca Dall'Oglio, eds. Bangkok, Thailand: UNESCO Principal Regional Office for Asia and the Pacific, pp. 15–117.

Mathew, Elangikal Thomas. 1997. *Employment and Unemployment in Kerala: Some Neglected Aspects*. Thousand Oaks, CA: Sage Publications.

Mortensen, Dale T. 1986. "Job Search and Labor Market Analysis." In *Handbook of Labor Economics*, Orley Ashenfelter and Richard Layard, eds. Amsterdam: North-Holland, pp. 849–919.

Mountford, Andrew. 1997. "Can a Brain Drain Be Good for Growth in the Source Economy?" *Journal of Development Economics* 53(2): 287–303.

Rogerson, Richard, Robert Shimer, and Randall Wright. 2005. "Search-Theoretic Models of the Labor Market." *Journal of Economic Literature* 43(4): 959–988.

Schaafsma, Joseph, and Arthur Sweetman. 2001. "Immigrant Earnings: Age at Immigration Matters." *Canadian Journal of Economics* 34(4): 1066–1099.

Srivastava, Ravi, and S.K. Sasikumar. 2003. "An Overview of Migration in

India, Its Impacts and Key Issues." Paper presented at the Regional Conference on Migration, Development, and Pro-Poor Policy Choices in Asia, held in Dhaka, Bangladesh, June 22–24.

Stark, Oded. 2004. "Rethinking the Brain Drain." *World Development* 32(1): 15–22.

Stark, Oded, Christian Helmenstein, and Alexia Prskawetz. 1997. "A Brain Gain with a Brain Drain." *Economics Letters* 55(2): 227–234.

———. 1998. "Human Capital Depletion, Human Capital Formation, and Migration: A Blessing or a 'Curse'?" *Economics Letters* 60(3): 363–367.

Stark, Oded, and Yong Wang. 2002. "Inducing Human Capital Formation: Migration as a Substitute for Subsidies." *Journal of Public Economics* 86(1): 29–46.

Todaro, Michael P. 1969. "A Model for Labor Migration and Urban Unemployment in Less Developed Countries." *American Economic Review* 59(1): 138–148.

Tullao, Tereso S., Jr. 1982. "Brain Drain, Education and Unemployment." *Philippines Budget Management* March–June(1982): 41–45.

4

How Does Migration
Affect Local Development?

What Mexico's Experience Tells Us

Christopher Woodruff
University of California, San Diego

Close to 200 million people live in a country other than that of their birth. Driven by large differences among countries in the wage rates paid to workers, the number of migrants worldwide continues to grow by about 3 percent a year. The largest share of these migrants move from developing to developed countries and have low to moderate education levels. A recent World Bank report (2005) estimates that in 2005 migrants returned $167 billion to their countries of origin.[1] Remittance flows have increased even more rapidly than migrant flows in recent years. According to the World Bank data, remittances more than quintupled between 1990 and 2005, an annual growth rate of 12 percent. The amount of remittances is now comparable to the flow of foreign direct investment and is about twice the size of foreign aid flows (World Bank 2005).

The 10 million Mexican migrants in the United States represent about 5 percent of the world migrant total. The $20 billion they sent home in 2005 represents more than 10 percent of world remittance transfers. As these measures underscore, the Mexico–United States migration pattern is surely the largest unilateral flow of people (in one direction) and resources (in the other) in the world.[2] For Mexico, migration to the United States is a significant economic and demographic phenomenon. Around 10 percent of individuals born in Mexico currently reside in the United States. The remittances these migrants send back to Mexico represent only about 2.5 percent of Mexico's national income. However, Mexican migration is geographically concentrated.

In some states, remittances represent more than 10 percent of income, and in some regions within states, a much higher percentage.

Both migration flows from Mexico and remittance flows to Mexico have grown rapidly in the past decade, mirroring international trends. The U.S. Census Bureau (2003) estimates that the Mexican-born population of the United States increased by 4.8 million during the 1990s and has continued to increase by 400,000 to 500,000 annually since. The Bank of Mexico (Banco de México 2007) estimates that remittances totaled $2.5 billion in 1990, $5.6 billion in 1998, and $20 billion in 2005, a 1990–2005 annual growth rate of 15 percent.

In what ways might these growing remittances affect the circumstances of households in sending countries (that is, countries that send migrants abroad)? Given the large sums flowing as remittances, it is easy to forget that remittances are actually large numbers of small flows: a typical recipient household in Mexico receives a few hundred dollars a month. This gives remittances a very different character from other international flows, such as foreign direct investment or international aid. Remittances flow to individuals, usually to those residing in households in the lower part of the income distribution. A growing number of researchers are examining the impact of remittances on household economic outcomes. I will summarize what we have learned from these studies and will also highlight an issue that makes isolating the impact of migration or remittances on the economies of sending countries very difficult.

MEASURING THE IMPACT OF MIGRATION

How can we measure the impact of migration on economic outcomes in sending countries? The simplest way would be to compare households with migrants and households without migrants. But in fact, such a comparison might be very misleading, because of the nature of migrants themselves. Migrants are not (or at least, are seldom) randomly selected from the population. For the most part, individuals, or individual households, choose to migrate, and others choose not to migrate, for a wide variety of reasons. Some characteristics that affect the likelihood of migrating are easy to measure. For instance, the relative returns to university education in Mexico are greater than in the United States. Thus, we might expect fewer individuals with a university education to migrate. This we can easily measure. But international migration involves risk—the risk of not finding a job and the risk of traveling, primarily. So less risk-averse individuals or households may also be more likely to migrate. However, risk aversion is difficult to measure, and it may affect a variety of other economic decisions and outcomes.

The connection between migrant households and the formation of microenterprises, an important element in the economies of sending nations, suggests the complex interplay of forces to be considered in analyzing the causes and effects of migration. If starting a household business requires capital, and if capital markets function poorly, then money earned abroad might be an important source of capital to start a business. In fact, data from the 2000 Mexican population census indicate that there is a strong connection between migration and the formation of microenterprises. Table 4.1 shows self-employment rates among household heads, both in households with and in households without migrants, as measured by the census.[3] In both urban and rural areas, and for both males and females, household heads are more likely to be self-employed in households with migrants.

Might this difference be caused by migration? Is it the result of remittance flows from migrants? Perhaps. But it also is possible that both migration and self-employment are caused by some third factor that is difficult to control for in making the comparison. Those who choose to migrate may have more energy and be more entrepreneurial than those who choose not to migrate. Those people who tend to be more entre-

Table 4.1 Self-Employment Rates in Mexico (%)

	With migrant in family	Without migrant in family
Urban males	36.8	27.4
Rural males	44.9	36.6
Urban females	38.0	26.8
Rural females	44.0	37.0

NOTE: Data are for adults aged 18–65. Sampling weights are used so that the sample represents all urban (population more than 100,000) and all rural (population less than 15,000) areas.

SOURCE: Mexican 2000 census population data.

preneurial may be both more likely to migrate and more likely to enter self-employment.

Untangling cause and effect is the challenge. Ideally, we would observe a group of identical individuals, some of whom migrate and some of whom do not. Differences between the groups would then be attributable to migration. However, except in a few cases where migrants in formal programs are chosen by lottery, this is not likely to be possible. So we have to look for alternative ways of finding appropriate subsets of the population to compare with migrants. In Mexico, I would argue, we can make use of the fact that migrants historically have come disproportionately from a certain region of the country. A key to identifying the impacts of migration on households in Mexico is that, at least historically, a handful of states in central-western Mexico have provided more than half of the migrants to the United States. I will refer to this region as the high-migration region. With some additional assumptions, we can compare outcomes of households in the high-migration region with outcomes of households in other, low-migration regions of Mexico.

Why do we need additional assumptions? Well, migration to another country requires some entrepreneurial initiative and a lot of energy. Sometimes people of a given region have a reputation for being particularly entrepreneurial. Before we compare households in the high-migration region with those in low-migration regions, we need to rule out the possibility that those in the high-migration region are not, collectively, more entrepreneurial or energetic.

There are two steps to eliminating this possibility. First, we need to ascertain that the differences in migration rates across regions are caused by factors other than differences in individual initiative. Here, understanding the origins of migration patterns is critical. Because early migration patterns are interesting and, it turns out, important to identifying the impacts of migration in Mexico, I will discuss them in some detail.

Second, even if differences in migration were caused by factors other than the characteristics of the people in the regions, we need to be sure that migration rates are not correlated by happenstance with characteristics that might lead to favorable economic outcomes.

In the 1990s, fully a third of the migrants to the United States came from one of three states in central-western Mexico: Jalisco, Michoacán, and Guanajuato (Rodríguez Ramírez 2003). Residents of these states were roughly twice as likely to migrate as the average Mexican. Just 1.5 percent of migrants came from the four states east of the Isthmus of Tehuantepec—Chiapas, Campeche, Yucatán, and Quintana Roo—which are home to 7 percent of the population.

Why did the central-western region of Mexico become such an important source of migrants? The answer turns out to be railroads. The first wave of migration from Mexico to the United States occurred early in the twentieth century. Demand for labor in the United States increased when migration from Europe slowed with the start of World War I. Many Mexican workers were recruited to help build rail lines in the southwestern United States. At the time, northern Mexico was scarcely populated. Thus, labor recruiters from the United States looked to the interior of Mexico. Recruiters chose as their destinations the interior states they could reach most quickly and at the lowest cost. These were the states accessible by rail.[4]

Figure 4.1 shows a map of Mexico with the major north-south rail lines as they existed around 1900. There were three major north-south rail lines in Mexico at that time, each built between 1884 and 1900. The first, the Central Mexican Railroad, went south from what is now Ciudad Juarez to Irapuato in the state of Guanajuato, where it branched east to Mexico City and west through Guadalajara to Colima near the Pacific Coast. In the north, the Central Mexican Railroad connected to the Southern Pacific and Texas Pacific railroads in Texas. A second line, the Mexican International Railroad, ran a shorter distance, from Durango through Chihuahua to Piedras Negras, then connected with the Southern Pacific in Eagle Pass, Texas. A third, the Mexican National Railroad, traveled north from Mexico City through San Luis Potosí and Monterrey, reaching the border at Nuevo Laredo, just across the Rio Grande from the southeastern Texas town of Laredo. This third line was less well connected to rail lines in the United States.

The state of Jalisco and its capital, Guadalajara, represented the closest area with a large population that was directly linked by rail. As a result, Guadalajara became the center of the high-migration region. By one estimate (Foerster 1925), 44 percent of migrants registering in Texas, Arizona, New Mexico, and California came from just three states in Mexico: Jalisco (20 percent), Michoacán (14 percent), and Guanajuato (10 percent). (In 1920, these four U.S. states were home to more than 90 percent of the Mexican-born population in the United

Figure 4.1 Major North-South Rail Lines in Mexico, circa 1900

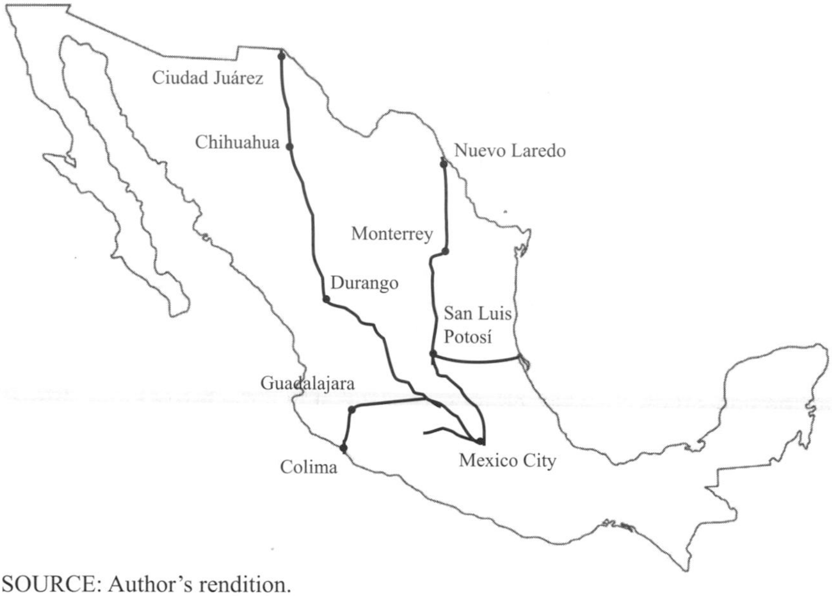

Ciudad Juárez

Chihuahua

Nuevo Laredo

Monterrey

Durango

San Luis Potosí

Guadalajara

Colima

Mexico City

SOURCE: Author's rendition.

States [Borjas and Katz 2005].) Another source puts the share of migrants to the United States coming from these three Mexican states at 33 percent over the 1926–1932 period (Durand, Massey, and Zenteno 2001). Foerster's 1924 data suggest that almost no migrants came from the states east of the isthmus of Tehuantepec; the present-day states of Chiapas, Campeche, Yucatán, and Quintana Roo were not connected by rail to the rest of Mexico and collectively accounted for less than 1 percent of the migrants in 1924.

Early migration was very highly correlated with distance to the railroad. The state-level correlation between distance to the rail lines and migration rates in the 1920s is 0.78. Of course, now few migrants travel to the United States by rail. Do the early rail lines remain an important factor in explaining the states of origin of migrants? The answer is yes. Early migrants provided information to others in their communities about opportunities for work in the United States. During the 1990s— long after railroads stopped being the main means of transportation north—the states of Jalisco, Michoacán, and Guanajuato remained the three states with the largest number of migrants going to the United States. Each accounted for about 11 percent of the national total, and collectively they accounted for 33.3 percent—almost exactly the same as the 33 percent share that Durand, Massey and Zenteno (2001) cite for the 1926–1932 period.[5] Overall, the state-level correlation between migration in the 1920s and migration in the second half of the 1990s is 0.43; the correlation between migration during the second half of the 1950s and the second half of the 1990s is 0.71. The early migrants established networks, which reproduced themselves.

Both the data and the historical accounts suggest that the early rail lines caused the central-western states in Mexico to become the most important source of migrants. This resulting pattern, consistent over decades, opens the possibility that comparing outcomes in high- and low-migration states might provide insights into the impact of migration on local development. But we don't quite yet have a convincing story. We must first address concerns that present-day differences between people in high- and low-migration regions may stem from factors other than migration. Perhaps people from the high-migration region are different merely by chance, and the differences themselves did not cause the migration. Or perhaps the rail lines caused differences in outcomes, not just in the migration that they facilitated. Researchers who have relied on differences in historical migration rates to identify the impacts of migration in Mexico have concluded that neither of these is the case. I leave the details of their evidence to later in the chapter, where I discuss their results. For now, I will say only that the data indicate that the high-migration states were, on average, poorer than low-migration states during the first half of the twentieth century. Hence, premigration measures of health, education, and income are lower in the high-migration regions. A finding that households in high-migration regions now have better outcomes implies that they have overcome this initial disadvantage. If anything, it appears that using historical migration regions as a laboratory to observe migration's economic effects is likely to provide a conservative estimate of the impacts of migration.

Remittances and Migration

The 2000 Mexico population census asks whether any member of the household has migrated outside of Mexico during the past five

58

Figure 4.2 Mexican Migration Rates by State, 1995–2000

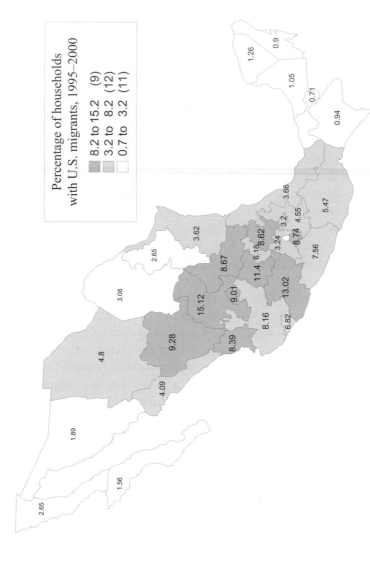

Percentage of households
with U.S. migrants, 1995–2000

▓ 8.2 to 15.2 (9)
▒ 3.2 to 8.2 (12)
☐ 0.7 to 3.2 (11)

NOTE: The rate for the Federal District is 2.05 percent.
SOURCE: Author's calculations using Mexican 2000 census population data.

years. Slightly less than 5 percent of households report having at least one migrant to the United States. Figure 4.2 shows a map of Mexico's 32 states, labeled with the percentage of households in the state that had migrants during the years between 1995 and 2000. The first column of Table 4.2 shows the same data. As noted above, there is significant variation in migration rates across states. Most of the high-migration states are located in central-western Mexico, with the highest rates being found in the states of Zacatecas (which has migration from 15.1 percent of households), Michoacán (13.0 percent), and Guanajuato (11.4 percent). States in southeastern Mexico have the lowest rates: Tabasco, Campeche, Yucatán, and Quintana Roo all have rates below 1.3 percent.

The census survey also asks whether members of the household have received money from family members living in another country. Just over 3 percent of households report that one or more members receive remittances. The percentage of individuals in each state receiving remittances is shown in column 2 of Table 4.2. At the state level, the correlation between migration and remittance rates in the 2000 census (columns 1 and 2 of Table 4.2) is 0.95.

What are the characteristics of households receiving remittances? Several patterns are apparent in the data. First, rural households are much more likely to receive remittances than urban households. Just under 5 percent of households in localities with fewer than 5,000 inhabitants report that they receive remittances, compared to just under 2 percent of households in urban areas with more than 100,000 inhabitants. By education level, the general pattern is that the lower the education level of the household head, the more likely the household is to receive remittances. Among households whose heads have five or fewer years of schooling, 5.3 percent report receiving remittances. Among those with six years of schooling, 3.1 percent say they receive remittances, and among those with 12 or more years of schooling, 1.2 percent report receiving remittances. The pattern in education is consistent with the fact that schooling attainment is lower in rural areas. At each schooling level, rural households are about twice as likely to receive remittances as are urban households.

Since there is a strong correlation between the schooling level of the household head and household income, we can say in sum that rural and lower-income households are more likely to receive remittances

**Table 4.2 State-Level Data on Households with Migrants and on
            Households Receiving Remittances (%)**

	Households w/ international migrants, 1995–2000	Households receiving remittances in 2000
Aguascalientes	9.01	4.90
Baja California	2.65	3.00
Baja California Sur	1.56	0.70
Campeche	1.05	0.70
Chiapas	0.94	0.50
Chihuahua	4.80	3.40
Coahuila	3.08	2.50
Colima	6.82	5.10
Distrito Federal	2.05	1.10
Durango	9.28	7.80
Guanajuato	11.40	6.90
Guerrero	7.56	5.80
Hidalgo	8.62	3.80
Jalisco	8.16	5.70
Mexico State	3.24	1.40
Michoacán	13.02	8.50
Morelos	8.74	4.60
Nayarit	8.39	6.80
Nuevo León	2.65	1.70
Oaxaca	5.47	3.00
Puebla	4.55	2.50
Querétaro	6.18	2.70
Quintana Roo	0.90	0.60
San Luis Potosí	8.67	6.30
Sinaloa	4.09	3.30
Sonora	1.89	2.20
Tabasco	0.71	0.40
Tamaulipas	3.62	2.70
Tlaxcala	3.20	1.60
Veracruz	3.66	2.00
Yucatán	1.26	1.00
Zacatecas	15.12	10.40

NOTE: Correlation of the percentage of households with migrants and the percentage
of households with remittances is 0.953. All averages are calculated using the factor
weights provided in the census to reproduce the population of each state.
SOURCE: Mexican 2000 census population data.

than are urban and higher-income households. Because rural and lower-income households are those most affected by infant mortality and early dropout rates, we might expect remittances to have an effect on these outcomes. And because self-employment in Mexico is strongly negatively correlated with schooling attainment, we might also expect remittances to affect the rate of self-employment. And, finally, if remittances raise household income, then the direct effect of remittances should tend to reduce income inequality.

Remittances or Migration?

Using the historical migration networks to identify an appropriate group of households to compare with migrant households helps to resolve the problem of endogeneity arising from missing information. But we should be careful about which effects we seek to identify through the historical migration networks. Briefly put, the historical networks allow us to identify the long-run impacts of migration on local development. By themselves, the historical migration networks don't allow us to separate the impact of remittances from other impacts related to migration. For example, migrants living abroad may gain knowledge or formal education that will affect their behavior when they return to their home country. This appears to be a part of the story where health outcomes are concerned.

Of course, remittances are likely to be the most important channel through which migration affects development. But they may not be the only channel. Even though the historical migration patterns are highly correlated with current remittance flows, when we use the historical migration in a two-stage least squares setup, we will identify only this long-run historical component. Identifying the impact of remittances per se will require a different instrument. For instance, short-run rainfall shocks might be expected to correlate with remittance flows; however, the rainfall shocks are likely to affect most of the other outcomes we are interested in measuring.

USING HISTORICAL MIGRATION NETWORKS TO IDENTIFY THE IMPACTS OF MIGRATION

Several researchers have used Mexico's historical migration networks to identify the impacts of migration on many different outcomes. I will focus the discussion here on three outcomes: capital for microenterprises, health, and education. With one exception, the authors I refer to claim to be identifying the impact of migration over the long term rather than the short term.

As the data in Table 4.1 indicate, self-employment is very common in Mexico. In urban areas, close to a quarter of the labor force is self-employed. The majority (about 60 percent) of these workers have no employees. The remaining 40 percent are split almost equally between those who "hire" only unpaid family workers and those who hire at least one paid-wage worker. The raw data in Table 4.1 appear to suggest that migration is associated with entry into self-employment, since percentages of those who are self-employed range from 7 to 11 percent higher in the four demographic categories if they have a migrant in the family.

Woodruff and Zenteno (2007) examine the impact of migration on microenterprises. Migration may affect either the supply of capital available to invest in microenterprises or the demand for products produced by microenterprises. (Massey and Parrado [1994] coined the term "migradollars" to describe the latter phenomenon.) Remittances flowing into a community increase the spending power of its residents. When asked how they spend remittances, respondents of most surveys indicate that 90 percent or more of the money is spent on current consumption (immediate needs). This spending increases demand for goods sold by local stores. Since about a third of microenterprises are involved in retail trade, migradollars may have a significant impact on the sales—and hence on the capital investments—of microenterprises.

In order to separate the demand-side and supply-side impacts of remittances on microenterprise investments, Woodruff and Zenteno (2007) focus on a group they refer to as internal migrants—the subset of individuals who reside in a Mexican state other than their state of birth. They argue that migration networks survive not only across time but across space as well. Using 2000 population census data, they show that people living in the same state are more likely to receive remittances if they were born in high-migration states rather than in low-migration states.

In other words, consider two households living in Mexico City, one whose head was born in Michoacán (high migration) and one whose head was born in Yucatán (low migration). The former is significantly more likely to receive remittances. Since these two individuals live in the same city, they face similar demand-side impacts from migradollars flowing into that city. But as the result of migration networks, they have different access to capital. Thus, by focusing on internal migrants, Woodruff and Zenteno (2007) are able to isolate the impact of migration on the supply of capital to microenterprises.

Examining first the effect of migration on the decision to be self-employed, Woodruff and Zenteno (2007) find no significant correlation between migration and entry into self-employment, instrumenting for migration with either the historical migration rates or with the distance of the state to the railroad network circa 1910. This suggests that the correlation found in Table 4.1 more likely reflects the fact that households that are more entrepreneurial are both more likely to have migrants and more likely to start an enterprise, and that migration has no causal effect on the formation of microenterprises in urban areas in Mexico.

However, Woodruff and Zenteno (2007) do find a clear and robust association between migration and the amount of capital invested in household enterprises. By their estimate, migration is causally associated with about one-quarter of all capital invested in microenterprises located in urban areas in Mexico. Table 4.3 shows the results they report on the impact of migration on investment in each of five investment categories. The largest effect is on vehicles. Since the authors are unable to separate returned migrants from those investing remittances sent by others, it is likely that part of this effect reflects the frequency with which migrants return to Mexico with a vehicle purchased in the United States. But investments in inventories and (more marginally) in tools and equipment are also significantly associated with migration.

The basic results provide support for the importance of remittances as a source of capital in microenterprises. But what effect does that capital have on the sales and earnings of the enterprises? Here the answer appears to differ according to the capital intensity of the sector. In high-capital sectors, migration is associated with higher investment,

Table 4.3 Log of Replacement Cost of Invested Capital by Type of Investment

	Real estate	Tools and equipment	Vehicles	Inventories	Other investments
Migration rate, state of birth	3.04 (0.85)	4.70 (1.69)	9.35 (2.38)	6.38 (2.00)	3.44 (1.01)
State fixed effects	Yes	Yes	Yes	Yes	Yes
Industry controls	Yes	Yes	Yes	Yes	Yes
Number of observations	1,675	1,675	1,675	1,675	1,675
R-squared	0.13	0.42	0.34	0.41	0.34

NOTE: t-values in parentheses. Standard errors are corrected for clustering at the state level for the state of birth. Sample limited to owners 18–65 years of age working at least 35 hours per week. The migration rate is instrumented with the distance from the north-south railway lines, as described in the text. In addition to the variables shown, all regressions include seven variables indicating the sector of activity. Other controls included in the regression are years of schooling of the owner, the estimated labor market experience (age minus years of schooling minus 6), the age of the firm in years, the square of each of these variables, a dummy indicating that the owner reports data for two enterprises, and the income per capita in the owner's state of birth.
SOURCE: Woodruff and Zenteno (2007).

higher sales, and higher profits. In low-capital sectors, there is a much smaller positive impact on investment and profits, and no impact on sales. These results suggest that remittances from migration relieve capital constraints where they are more likely to bind—in high-capital sectors. But enterprises in low-capital sectors might be viewed as a place to stash the liquidity coming from migration, without generating such dramatic effects on the operation of the enterprise.

Hildebrandt and McKenzie (2005) are interested in the impact of migration on child health outcomes in Mexico. Here, the methodological problem they encounter is that healthier families may be more likely to migrate, hence a positive correlation between healthy children and migration may be the result of causation in either direction. To avoid this problem, the authors use state-level historical migration data as an instrument for current migration. Yet they still must address the concern that historical migration is associated either positively or negatively with contemporaneous health conditions. However, they find that migration rates in 1924 are not significantly correlated with child mortality rates in 1930, the earliest date for which such data are available.

They also find that historical migration rates are largely uncorrelated with measures of health services in 1996.

Hildebrandt and McKenzie find that migration has a large and significant impact on the well-being of children in Mexico. They use data from the 1997 Mexican demographic survey of households known as ENADID, which includes information on whether anyone from the household has ever migrated.[6] Because they are interested in the impact of migration on children after the act of migration, they define migrant households as those households with at least one migrant going to the United States before the beginning of 1994, and nonmigrant households as those with no migrants or later migrants. Hildebrandt and McKenzie report positive effects of migration on the health of children in Mexico once the endogeneity of migration is taken into account. The effects are large. Migration is associated with about a 3.0-percentage-point reduction in the probability of a baby dying in the first year of life, and an increase in birth weight of 350 grams, or around 0.8 pounds. The authors' OLS results suggest no significant correlation between migration and health. The lack of significance in the OLS regressions combined with the significant positive outcomes found in the instrumental variable regressions together suggest that the positive health outcomes themselves make migration less likely. Not all of the impacts of migration on children's health are positive, however. Children born in migrant households are less likely to be vaccinated or to see doctors during the first year of their lives. Hildebrandt and McKenzie attribute this to greater time demands on the parent because of migration from the household.

The findings of Hildebrandt and McKenzie are corroborated by López Córdoba (2005), who uses *municipio* (county) level data from the 2000 Mexican population census to examine the impact of migration and remittances on health and education. López Córdoba attempts to separate the impact of migration from the impact of remittances by using historical migration to control for migration and by using current remittance flows to measure remittances.[7] Because historical migration rates are available only at the state level, López Córdoba proxies for historical migration by measuring the distance from each municipio to the nearest rail line existing in the 1920s, plus the distance from that point to the border. Since most migrants—and labor recruiters—traveled by rail at that time, the distance proxies for the cost of migration. López Córdoba also includes a measure of the percentage of households in each municipio that reported receiving remittances in 2000. His claim is, then, that the distance variable accounts for long-run impacts of migration and allows for the isolation of the impact of current remittance flows, through the remittance variable. López Córdoba finds that infant mortality is decreasing in the share of households receiving remittances and increasing in the historical cost of migration. The latter implies again that migration is negatively associated with infant mortality rates, since migration itself falls as migration costs rise. López Córdoba focuses his discussion on the magnitude of the effect of remittances, which appears to be about a third of the magnitude of the effect reported by Hildebrandt and McKenzie.

There is slightly more disagreement with respect to migration's effect on educational attainment, but a general picture emerges from several studies addressing this issue. Several issues make understanding the impact of migration on education particularly difficult. For one thing, most databases organize individuals by households. As early as age 16, children begin to split off to form their own households, or, more frequently, join the household of a relative in another city. Tracking the individual to the remittance behavior of the household then becomes impossible. Also, in urban areas, at earlier ages the children's schooling attainment and attendance do not vary much, because primary schooling is universal in urban Mexico and lower secondary schooling is nearly so.

With this in mind, Hanson and Woodruff (2003) study educational attainment in rural areas in Mexico among children 10–14 years of age. An issue for the analysis of dynamics in rural regions is that households seldom move from rural areas in one state to rural areas in another state. Thus, the strategy Woodruff and Zenteno (forthcoming) use to separate high-migration households and high-migration states is not available to Hanson and Woodruff. Instead, Hanson and Woodruff juxtapose the historical migration rates with household characteristics that are associated with migration, such as age and education of the mother. They find that migration has a positive effect on schooling in households in which the female head has two or fewer years of schooling. About a third of households in rural areas have female heads with two or fewer years of schooling. Among the two-thirds of the rural households in which the female head has higher levels of schooling, Hanson and Woodruff find a significant effect only among 10- to 12-year-old boys.

McKenzie and Rapoport (2006) use the ENADID 1997 survey in Mexico to examine the impact of migration on schooling outcomes among 12- to 18-year-olds in localities with populations below 50,000. They find that migration has a negative effect on schooling for both boys and girls 16–18 years of age, and a negative effect among boys aged 12–15. Hanson and Woodruff also find a negative effect among boys aged 13–15 whose mothers have three or more years of schooling. Among girls of the same age, Hanson and Woodruff find a positive, significant effect where mothers have low schooling and a negative, insignificant effect where mothers have three or more years of schooling. McKenzie and Rapoport attribute the negative effects of migration on schooling among 16- to 18-year-olds to a low return on education (since education obtained in Mexico has a low value in labor markets in the United States) and to higher opportunity costs caused by missing household members. However, it may also be the case that continuing on to high school requires moving out of the household to a city, since high schools are not common in rural areas. The question then is whether those who have stayed in school and left the household are reported as regular members of the household. If they are, then the results suggest a strong negative impact of migration on educational attainment at higher levels.

Finally, McKenzie and Rapoport (2004) examine the broader impacts of migration on income inequality in Mexico, again using historical migration as a means of identifying the impacts. They reach the interesting conclusion that migration initially increases inequality, because the cost of migration means that the poorest households do not migrate. However, once migration networks are established in a community, the costs of migrating fall. Members of poorer households then migrate with more frequency, and inequality is reduced.

Most of the issues addressed in the research on impacts of migration—health, education, and capital for household enterprises—are particularly acute problems among the lower-income households in Mexico. With the exception of the suggestion that migration may have a negative impact on high school education, the research indicates that migration has a positive impact on economic outcomes in each of these areas. Since, as was noted earlier, remittances flow to lower-income (as measured by the schooling attainment of the head) and rural households, this suggests that over the longer term, we should expect remittances to reduce income inequality in Mexico.

CONCLUSION

I have focused on the impacts of migration from a single country, Mexico. Households with members who migrate abroad are likely to differ in systematic ways from households without migrants. The difficulty in measuring all of the ways in which these two groups of households differ presents a challenge for those attempting to identify the impacts of migration on sending countries. Is an observed difference the result of migration, or is it the cause of migration? Absent a strategy for identifying an appropriate comparison group, this is a difficult question to answer. For much of the past half-century, development economists have been primarily concerned with the negative impacts of migration on sending countries, such as brain drain. But an increasing number of studies examining diverse outcomes in Mexico are showing that migration has positive impacts there. Taken together, the studies also suggest that migration's effects are complex. In Mexico, it appears that educational attainment increases for younger children but decreases for older children. Child mortality appears to decrease with migration, but so do visits to doctors and vaccinations. Self-employment rates in urban areas remain unchanged, but the level of capital investment in enterprises and the earnings derived from those enterprises increase.

Whether migration has similar effects in other sending countries is unclear. What is clear is that the best strategies for untangling these effects will vary from country to country and will take advantage of circumstances that allow for new insights into the phenomenon of remittances. The key is not the specific instrument used to separate cause and effect, but the identification of an appropriate instrument for a given region or country. In Mexico, historical migration patterns are useful vehicles for comparison. In other countries, researchers have devised other novel strategies. One example of this is provided by Yang's (2004) work measuring the impact of remittances in the Philippines. Yang uses the devaluation of Asian currencies in 1997–1998 to identify the impacts of remittances on economic outcomes. This strategy is specific to the Philippines, whose migrants are dispersed around the globe. The devaluation of many Asian currencies in the 1997–1998 period provided a nice natural shock to remittance flows into the Philippines: the Philippine peso value of remittances from migrants to the United States, or to Middle Eastern countries paying wages in dollars, increased when the Philippine currency was devalued. But since the Korean, Thai, and other Asian currencies were devalued at the same time, the remittances of workers in those countries did not similarly increase.

It is not possible to exploit this kind of variation in Mexico or Central America, where the vast majority of migrants go to a single country, the United States. However, isolation of the impacts of migration in Mexico, an important sending country, is possible because patterns of historical migration allow us to identify an appropriate comparison group against which to measure the progress of migrant households.

Most of the issues addressed in the research on impacts of migration—health, education, and capital for household enterprises—are particularly acute problems among the lower-income households in Mexico. With the exception of the suggestion that migration may have a negative impact on high school education, the research indicates that migration has a positive impact on economic outcomes. Since remittances flow to lower-income (as measured by the schooling attainment of the head) and rural households, this suggests that over the long term we should expect remittances to contribute to a reduction of income inequality in Mexico.

Notes

1. Remittance flows are sometimes divided into three categories: compensation for workers, remittances, and migrant transfers. The first two are differentiated by the length of time the worker is resident in the destination country and whether he or she is considered a resident there. Both of these are captured as current flows in the balance of payments. The third category is captured on the capital account side of balance of payments. Since governments often have a difficult time identifying current flows with precision, the sum of the three categories is likely to be more accurate than the individual categories. Even so, we should recognize that remittance flows are difficult to track and that the data provided are only estimates.
2. As of 2000, only Russia (12.2 million) had more emigrants than Mexico (10.1 million), according to estimates (Parsons et al. 2005). About 95 percent of mi-

grants from Mexico live in the United States, while the Russian diaspora is more dispersed geographically.

3. The census distinguishes between households with and households without migrants by asking whether anyone in the household has migrated during the past five years—that is, between 1995 and 2000.

4. Railroads were the only practical means for traveling long distances over land in Mexico in the early 1900s. According to Coatsworth (1972, pp. 86–93), stagecoach travel in 1910 was three times as costly and was only one-fifth as fast.

5. Estimates by state vary slightly, but one reasonable estimate based on Mexican census data suggests that during the 1990s 11.1 percent came from Guanajuato, 11.2 percent from Jalisco, and 11.0 percent from Michoacán (Rodríguez Ramírez 2003).

6. The survey is conducted at five-year intervals. ENADID stands for Encuesta Nacional de la Dinámica Demográfica, or National Survey on Demographic Dynamics.

7. López Córdoba uses the coefficient of variation in historical monthly rainfall as an instrument for current remittance receipts. He argues that higher variation in rainfall within the year gives rise to a greater need for consumption-smoothing strategies, including remittances.

References

Banco de México. 2007. *Búsqueda General*. Mexico City: Banco de México. http://www.banxico.org.mx/AplBusquedasBM2/busqwww2.jsp?_action =search (accessed March 30, 2007).

Borjas, George J., and Lawrence F. Katz. 2005. "The Evolution of the Mexican-Born Workforce in the United States." NBER Working Paper No. 11281. Cambridge, MA: National Bureau of Economic Research.

Coatsworth, John H. 1972. "The Impact of Railroads on the Economic Development of Mexico, 1877–1910." PhD dissertation, University of Wisconsin.

Durand, Jorge, Douglas S. Massey, and Rene M. Zenteno. 2001. "Mexican Immigration in the United States: Continuities and Changes." *Latin American Research Review* 36(1): 107–127.

Foerster, Robert F. 1925. *The Racial Problems Involved in Immigration from Latin America and the West Indies to the United States*. Washington, DC: U.S. Department of Labor.

Hanson, Gordon H., and Christopher Woodruff. 2003. "Emigration and Educational Attainment in Mexico." Working paper. San Diego: University of California, San Diego, Graduate School of International Relations and Pacific Studies.

Hildebrandt, Nicole, and David McKenzie. 2005. "The Effects of Migration on Child Health in Mexico." *Economia* 6(1): 257–289.

López Córdoba, Ernesto. 2005. "Globalization, Migration, and Development: The Role of Mexican Migrant Remittances." *Economia* 6(1): 217–256.

Massey, Douglas S., and Emilio Parrado. 1994. "Migradollars: The Remittances and Savings of Mexican Migrants to the USA." *Population Research and Policy Review* 13(1): 3–30.

McKenzie, David, and Hillel Rapoport. 2004. "Network Effects and the Dynamics of Migration and Inequality: Theory and Evidence from Mexico." BREAD Working Paper No. 063. Cambridge, MA: Bureau for Research on Economic Analysis of Development, Harvard University.

———. 2006. "Can Migration Reduce Educational Attainment? Evidence from Mexico." World Bank Policy Research Working Paper No. 3952. Washington, DC: World Bank.

Parsons, Christopher R., Ronald Skeldon, Terrie L. Walmsley, and L. Alan Winters. 2005. "Quantifying the International Bilateral Movements of Migrants." Working Paper T13. Brighton, Sussex, UK: Development Research Centre on Migration, Globalisation and Poverty, University of Sussex.

Rodríguez Ramírez, Héctor. 2003. "Tendencias Recientes de la Migración Internacional y las Remesas en Coahuila." *Revista Region y Sociedad* 15(28): 127–160.

U.S. Census Bureau. 2003. *The Foreign-Born Population: 2000.* Census 2000 Brief. C2KBR-34. Washington, DC: U.S. Department of Commerce, Economics and Statistics Administration, U.S. Census Bureau. http://www.census.gov/prod/2003pubs/c2kbr-34.pdf (accessed March 29, 2007).

Woodruff, Christopher, and Rene Zenteno. 2007. "Migration Networks and Microenterprises in Mexico." *Journal of Development Economics* 82(2): 509–528.

World Bank. 2005. *Global Economic Prospects 2006: Economic Implications of Remittances and Migration.* Washington: World Bank.

Yang, Dean. 2004. "International Migration, Human Capital, and Entrepreneurship: Evidence from Philippine Migrants' Exchange Rate Shocks." Gerald R. Ford School of Public Policy Working Paper No. 02-011. Ann Arbor, MI: University of Michigan.

5
Remittance Patterns of Latin American Immigrants in the United States

Catalina Amuedo-Dorantes
San Diego State University

Migrant remittances, defined as transfers of funds from migrants in the United States to relatives or friends in their country of origin, have increasingly attracted the attention of policymakers as the large amounts of money involved and the role of remittances in economic development have become more evident. Indeed, at a macroeconomic level, remittances constitute one of the largest and least volatile sources of foreign exchange in many developing economies. The magnitude of these remittance flows is only expected to rise, given the increasing out-migration experienced by many of these regions. As noted by de Vasconcelos (2005) of the Inter-American Development Bank, nowhere is this movement of workers and funds more important than in Latin America and the Caribbean, where domestic incomes and capital flows have been drying up following periods of economic crisis. Remittances from the United States to Latin American and Caribbean nations totaled more than $40 billion in 2004. This amount exceeded the combined flows of all foreign direct investment (FDI) and net official development assistance (ODA) to the region. De Vasconcelos goes on to note that the volume of remittances received by the Latin American and Caribbean countries is now the highest and fastest growing of any region in the world. Remittances surpass tourism income in each country of that region, account for at least 10 percent of the gross domestic product (GDP) in six countries, and almost always exceed a country's largest export.

Perhaps the most popular task of economists studying the remittance market in recent years has been the measurement of these flows.

In addition, the literature has tried to gain a better understanding of migrants' remitting patterns and the microeconomic impacts of these patterns by examining who is likely to remit, for what purposes, and how remittances are ultimately used by the receiving families. Yet the lack of comparable survey instruments has impeded the completion of interesting cross-country comparisons that would shed some light on the role of socioeconomic, political, and cultural differences in explaining migrants' remittance patterns and how their families and friends ultimately use the funds they send back home.

In this chapter, I use two surveys—the Mexican Migration Project and the Latin American Migration Project—designed to measure migration and migrants' remitting patterns across several countries. The similitude of these two survey instruments allows for a comparative analysis. In particular, it permits us to uncover country-level similarities and differences that are key in devising policies to facilitate these money flows and maximize their potential for improving the livelihood of migrants' families back home.

DATA

The Mexican Migration Project (MMP93) reports only on Mexico, whereas the Latin American Migration Project (LAMP) reports on Costa Rica, the Dominican Republic, Haiti, Nicaragua, and Peru.[1] The LAMP is a companion project to the MMP93, which was begun in 1982 to study the migration patterns of Mexicans within Mexico as well as Mexicans who have come to the United States. The MMP93 database includes detailed social, demographic, and economic information from approximately 16,000 households in 93 representative communities in 17 of Mexico's 31 states.[2] The MMP93 survey was carried out annually in the winter months of 1982–1983 and 1987–2002.[3] For each household, a complete life history is gathered on the household head, including detailed information on past migration experiences in the United States (number and duration of trips, documentation used, etc.). After gathering information on these households, interviewers travel to the destination areas in the United States to administer identical questionnaires to households from the same communities in Mexico; these immigrants have settled in the United States and no longer return home. Altogether, the 5,837 immigrants surveyed in the MMP93 constitute a reasonably representative data set on authorized and unauthorized Mexican immigrants in the United States (Amuedo-Dorantes, Bansak, and Pozo 2005; Massey and Zenteno 2000; Munshi 2003).

The LAMP uses the same methodology as the MMP93 to expand our knowledge of migration in a variety of countries in Latin America and the Caribbean. So far, only one wave of data is available—that wave having been collected between 1999 and 2003, depending on the country under consideration. Because of this, when I explore house-hold remittance-receiving patterns, I work with data from approximate-ly 1,400 households from Costa Rica, a little under 1,000 households from the Dominican Republic, about 300 households from Haiti, almost 1,800 households in Nicaragua, and close to 700 households from Peru. When investigating immigrants' remitting patterns, I rely on data from approximately 192 immigrants from Costa Rica, 166 immigrants from the Dominican Republic, 36 immigrants from Haiti, 161 immigrants from Nicaragua, and 61 immigrants from Peru.

MIGRATION AS THE PRECONDITION TO REMITTANCES

To the extent that remittances are money transfers from emigrants of a country to friends and relatives back in their countries of origin, these flows are conditional on the out-migration patterns of the receiv-ing economies. As such, it is illuminating to ask the following ques-tions about emigrants from each of these countries: What percentage of emigrants from these economies enter illegally into the United States? What percentage rely on smugglers to help them cross the border? How much do migrants pay, on average, for the smugglers' services? Has the cost significantly increased during the past decade? Finally, how many trips do legal and unauthorized migrants in each of these coun-tries make to the United States, on average?

These questions all provide us with valuable information likely to influence remittance payments. For instance, countries with a higher proportion of unauthorized immigrants in the United States may be more likely to receive larger remittance flows. After all, unauthorized immigrants are exposed to higher income risks and, as such, may be more likely to remit money back home as an insurance mechanism in case the migration experience turns out to be unsuccessful (Amuedo-Dorantes and Pozo 2006). Likewise, the broad use of smuggling services is likely to make the migratory experience more expensive. The debt incurred often means that migrants must pay back immediate family and relatives for funding their trip. Alternatively, migrants may have to foot the expenses for additional family members to come (Ilahi and Jafarey 1999). Finally, frequent trips back home may also influence how much money is remitted home on a periodic basis as opposed to being brought back home at the end of the migration experience (Bauer and Sinning 2005).

Figures 5.1–5.3 and Tables 5.1A and 5.1B provide some combined migration statistics for all the countries included in this study as well as separate statistics for each country. Approximately 68 percent of the 6,392 Latin American immigrants in the study, or about 4,350, are unauthorized.[4] Additionally, about 75 percent of illegal border crossers use smuggling services. Figures 5.1 and 5.2 show these same categories broken down by immigrants' country of origin. Mexico is the country

Figure 5.1 Percentage of Unauthorized Immigrants, by Country

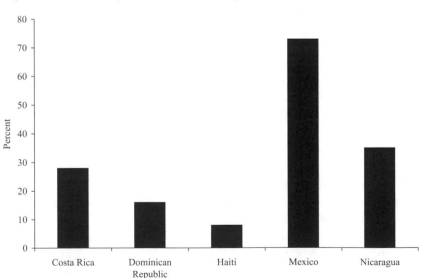

SOURCE: Author's tabulations using the MMP93 and the LAMP.

Figure 5.2 Percentage of Unauthorized Immigrants Using Smugglers, by Country

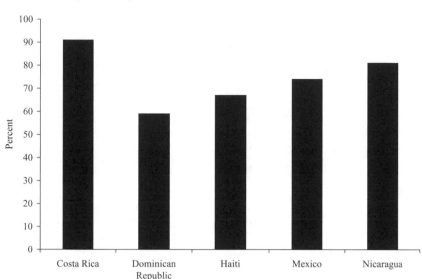

SOURCE: Author's tabulations using the MMP93 and the LAMP.

we are most familiar with in this respect, given the predominance of Mexicans among all other immigrant groups in the United States. The percentage of unauthorized immigrants from Mexico is more than twice as high as the percentage from Nicaragua, the country with the next highest percentage of illegals. This may possibly be explained by the greater distance to be traveled in the case of Costa Rica and Nicaragua, and the hazards of sea travel in the case of Haiti and the Dominican Republic. Additionally, an even higher percentage of unauthorized immigrants rely on the services provided by smugglers in Costa Rica (91 percent) and Nicaragua (81 percent) than do so in Mexico (74 percent). As such, the possibility exists that Costa Ricans and Nicaraguans remit substantial sums of money back home, either to pay back their own travel loans or to finance the comparatively more expensive trips of relatives. The lowest usage of smuggling is found among immigrants from the Dominican Republic. Because only a small number of observations are available for this country, it is difficult to ascertain why such low rates occur here. However, the lower use of smuggling services

Figure 5.3 Average Number of Border Crossings per Migrant, by Documentation Status and Use of Smuggling Services

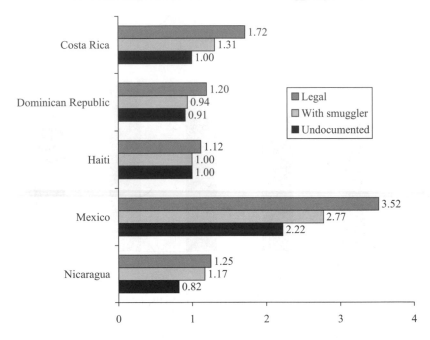

SOURCE: Author's tabulations using the MMP93 and the LAMP.

by Dominicans could be, in part, related to the lower realized success rate of smuggler-aided crossings among Dominicans in the survey compared to the rate for unauthorized Dominicans who choose not to rely on these services.

We also have information on the average number of crossings for legal versus unauthorized immigrants in each of the countries being surveyed (Figure 5.3). As we would expect, legal immigrants make a larger number of U.S. visits—three on average—than do unauthorized immigrants, who average two to almost three.[5] Therefore, we would expect unauthorized immigrants to remit more money to their families than legal immigrants, who can more easily return home and bring money back to their families in person.

Tables 5.1A and 5.1B give the cost in U.S. dollars to unauthorized immigrants of using smuggling services. Unauthorized immigrants are a group that carries special interest given their potentially higher likelihood of remitting larger proportions of their earnings back home. Only 62 percent of illegal border crossers using smugglers report on the cost incurred from using their services. On average, these unauthorized immigrants report paying $427 for each crossing. This cost was as low as $303 during the 1990s and increased to an average of $633 from 2000 onwards. Table 5.1A also shows how immigrants' use of smuggling services is inversely related to the cost of such services, thus suggesting the existence of a downward sloping demand for smuggling services on the part of unauthorized immigrants. Table 5.1B reveals large variation by country in smuggling costs. Mexican immigrants, at an average cost per trip of about $370, pay the least for smuggling services, which is to be expected because of the geographic proximity of Mexico to the United States. In contrast, Costa Rica, the most distant country from the United States in the sample under consideration, has the highest average amount paid by its emigrants for smuggling services (about $2,100). The average price paid by Nicaraguans is approximately $1,700, whereas Dominicans pay about $1,000. Given the limited number of observations available for some of these countries, it is difficult to clearly identify trends. However, if we focus on those countries for which there are a larger number of observations—Mexico, Nicaragua, and Costa Rica—it appears as if smuggling costs have been

Table 5.1A Average Cost of Smuggling Services and Its Relationship to Successful Crossings, All Countries ($)

	N	Mean	Std. dev.
Average cost	2,034	426.74	584.62
Average cost by decade of last U.S. visit			
During 1990s	1,273	303.25	408.88
2000 and later	761	633.33	752.45
Average cost by number of successful crossings			
None	11	815.23	1,417.40
One	1,050	462.53	662.59
Two	498	393.57	489.86
Three	266	362.03	423.58

SOURCE: Author's tabulations using the MMP93 and the LAMP.

Table 5.1B Average Cost of Smuggling Services and Its Relationship to Successful Crossings, by Immigrants' Country of Origin ($)

	Costa Rica			Dominican Republic			Haiti			Nicaragua			Mexico		
Variable	N	Mean	Std. dev.	N	Mean	Std. dev.	N	Mean	Std. dev.	N	Mean	Std. dev.	N	Mean	Std. dev.
Average cost	32	2,101.56	1,223.72	13	1,035.58	977.21	2	4,000.00	2,828.43	36	1,670.60	1,298.21	1,961	368.60	445.54
Average cost by decade of last U.S. visit															
During 1990s	11	1,022.73	611.30	7	1,090.29	1,322.55	1	6,000.00	—	27	1,401.54	981.53	1,227	263.50	280.38
2000 and later	21	2,666.67	1,076.49	6	971.75	527.80	1	2,000.00	—	9	2,477.78	1,806.95	724	546.73	592.92
Average cost of smuggling services by number of successful crossings															
None	0	—	—	1	1,130.00	—	0	—	—	0	—	—	10	783.75	1,490.01
One	24	1,981.25	1,172.22	11	962.05	1,065.57	2	4,000.00	2,828.43	29	1,279.02	1,327.38	984	375.38	476.43
Two	6	2,158.33	1,473.32	1	1,750.00	—	—	—	—	7	1,428.57	1,234.52	484	353.92	381.79
Three	1	3,000.00	—	—	—	—	—	—	—	—	—	—	265	352.08	391.97

NOTE: — = not available.
SOURCE: Author's tabulations using the MMP93 and the LAMP.

on the rise since the 1990s. In the cases of Mexico and Costa Rica, these costs have more than doubled. The increasing cost of smuggling services may have heightened the need on the part of immigrants to remit money home, both to pay their debt and to finance the migration of additional household members to the United States. It is interesting to note how the downward-sloping demand for smuggling services on the part of unauthorized immigrants suggested by Table 5.1A is supported by the Mexican data in Table 5.1B. However, in the case of Costa Ricans or Nicaraguans, a larger number of successful illegal border crossings is directly linked to a higher cost for smuggling services. As such, these migrants may be "getting what they paid for."

IMMIGRANTS' REMITTING PATTERNS: HOW MUCH IS SENT? BY WHOM? FOR WHAT PURPOSES?

How Much?

Perhaps the most basic yet difficult task of remittance researchers has been to measure these money flows and the percentage of immigrants sending money back home. Table 5.2 provides a comparison of such figures across the countries being examined. More than 5,700 immigrants, or about 89 percent of immigrants in the sample, provide information regarding their remitting practices. Approximately 70 percent of those 5,703 immigrants report that they sent money back home on a monthly basis during their last U.S. trip. This figure is in line with the more than 60 percent of immigrants from Nicaragua, Costa Rica, the Dominican Republic, Mexico, and Haiti that remit money home. In contrast, only 46 percent of the 52 Peruvian immigrants in the sample sent money home to their families on a monthly basis.

Table 5.2 also lists the average dollar amounts remitted home by immigrants from these Latin American and Caribbean nations. These average $300 a month, or 40 percent of immigrants' income. Money transfers are smallest among immigrants from the Dominican Republic ($179 a month) and largest among immigrants from Costa Rica ($493). In line with this, Dominicans remit approximately 16 percent of their monthly earnings, whereas Costa Ricans remit about 55 percent. How-

Table 5.2 Remittance Patterns for Surveyed Latin American Countries

	Share of migrants remitting	Average amount remitted ($)	As a share of income
All countries			
Mean	0.71	301.68	0.40
Std. dev.	0.46	418.48	0.98
N	5,703	4,034	3,270
Costa Rica			
Mean	0.69	492.91	0.55
Std. dev.	0.46	865.46	1.00
N	167	115	78
Dominican Republic			
Mean	0.67	179.18	0.16
Std. dev.	0.47	195.31	0.21
N	154	103	84
Haiti			
Mean	0.74	284.56	0.13
Std. dev.	0.45	251.78	0.06
N	19	14	7
Nicaragua			
Mean	0.61	223.18	0.22
Std. dev.	0.49	255.03	0.35
N	132	80	61
Peru			
Mean	0.46	376.55	0.16
Std. dev.	0.50	371.75	0.14
N	52	24	12
Mexico			
Mean	0.71	300.43	0.41
Std. dev.	0.45	403.35	1.00
N	5,179	3,698	3,028

SOURCE: Author's tabulations using the MMP93 and the LAMP.

ever, there is not always a direct relationship between the dollar amount remitted and the percentage of monthly earnings remitted home. For instance, while the average dollar amount remitted by Peruvians is above the mean for the group of countries being examined, the percentage of income remitted by Peruvians is far below—they remit only 16 percent of their monthly earnings, compared to 41 percent for the other nationalities in the sample.

By Whom?

In addition to measuring remittance transfers, the literature has long examined immigrants' remitting motives. Overall, a variety of reasons for sending money back home has been identified, including altruism, exchange, investment, and coinsurance. The altruism motive suggests that remittance payments made by migrants to their families increase with the needs of household members back home (Becker 1974). The exchange motive, or at least the most predominant one, comes from existing evidence of immigrants repaying family members and friends back home for financing their trip (Cox 1987). Another motive, investment, occurs when immigrants remit money back home to purchase assets with the intent of earning an economic return. And Lucas and Stark (1985) call attention to yet another motive for sending money back home—coinsurance, by which both immigrants and family members or friends provide monetary and in-kind transfers to insure each other against economic shocks.

For What Purposes?

The MMP93 and LAMP ask remitters their purpose in sending money back home. Remitters are allowed to choose up to five motives for transferring money home. For practical purposes, these motives can be grouped into either "consumption" or "asset accumulation/investment," depending on whether remittances are sent by immigrants to cover the consumption needs of family and friends back home or to be invested in productive activities. Whether a particular expenditure category should constitute consumption or asset accumulation is debatable, particularly when it comes to assets such as housing. However, for the purposes of this study, I group the following motives under the category of asset accumulation: construction or repair of house, purchase of a house or lot, purchase of tools, purchase of livestock, purchase of agricultural inputs, start-up or expansion of a business, educational expenses, health expenses, and savings. In contrast, consumption comprises the following expenditures: food and maintenance, purchase of a vehicle, purchase of consumer goods, financing a special event, recreation/entertainment expenses, and debt payments. Figure 5.4 addresses migrants' remitting motives. Because migrants can indicate up to five motives for remitting money back home, the percentages of migrants sending money for consumption and asset accumulation purposes do not add up to 100. According to Figure 5.4, consumption is the overwhelming purpose behind immigrants' remitting practices, yet a nontrivial portion of remitters specify asset accumulation as a reason for sending money home.

Figure 5.4 Percentage of Immigrants That Remit for Consumption and Asset Accumulation

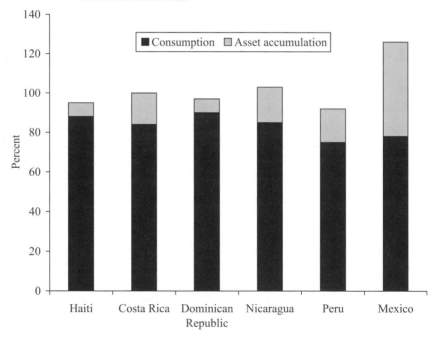

NOTE: Percentages do not add up to 100 because more than one purpose may be reported.
SOURCE: Author's tabulations using the MMP93 and the LAMP.

Consumption appears to be a more pressing remittance motive for immigrants coming from the Dominican Republic, Haiti, Peru, Nicaragua, and Costa Rica than it does for those from Mexico: only a small fraction of immigrants from those economies (never more than 18 percent of remitters) indicate sending money back home for asset accumulation purposes.

Several empirical studies have noted that remittances differ according to immigrants' age, family responsibilities back home, earnings, and whether they have temporary or permanent status (de la Garza and Lowell 2002; Taylor 1999). In addition to these characteristics, Tables 5.3 through 5.6 examine the variability of immigrants' remitting patterns and purposes according to whether or not the immigrants were authorized upon entry, their educational attainment, decade of visit, and area of residence while in the United States. Several findings are worth discussing. The data in Table 5.3 confirm what was hypothesized earlier in the chapter: that a higher percentage of unauthorized immigrants (75 percent) remit money back home than legal migrants do (64 percent). Yet the data in Table 5.4 indicate that there is not much difference in the percentage of earnings that these two groups of immigrants remit home.

Likewise, less educated immigrants appear more likely to remit than their more educated counterparts (59 percent compared to 50 percent in Table 5.3). There are no statistically significant differences among countries in how likely less educated immigrants are to remit relative to more educated immigrants. Nor do less educated immigrants seem to send a significantly higher proportion of their incomes home than more educated immigrants (20 versus 17 percent, Table 5.4).

Other interesting results refer to remittance trends. According to the data in Table 5.3, a higher percentage of Latin American immigrants have transferred money to their families during the present decade than in the 1990s. This is the case for Costa Ricans, Dominicans, Nicaraguans, Peruvians, and Mexicans; the exception is Haitians. However, the limited number of observations for Haiti casts doubt on any conclusions. Furthermore, Table 5.4 indicates that, as a percentage of migrants' monthly earnings, remittance transfers have also been on the rise among Dominicans and Peruvians during the current decade.

A final aspect revealed by Tables 5.3 and 5.4 involves changes in remitting patterns according to whether immigrants resided in a large

Table 5.3 Percentage of Migrants Remitting, by Documentation Status, Education, Decade, and City Dweller

Variable	All countries		Costa Rica		Dominican Republic		Haiti		Nicaragua		Peru[a]		Mexico	
	%	t-stat.	%	t-stat.	%	t-stat.	%	t-stat.	%	t-stat.	%	t-stat.	%	t-stat.
By documentation status														
Legal	0.64	—	0.66	—	0.68	—	0.69	—	0.57	—	0.44	—	0.66	—
Unauthorized	0.75	-8.36***	0.80	-1.76*	0.57	0.75	1.00	-2.61**	0.80	-2.22**	1.00	-7.90***	0.75	-7.34***
By educational attainment														
Up to 15 years	0.59	—	0.60	—	0.69	—	0.75	—	0.56	—	0.56	—	0.58	—
16+ years	0.50	2.37**	0.33	1.48	0.73	-0.35	0.50	0.48	0.53	0.29	0.37	1.29	0.50	1.44
By decade of visit														
During 1990s	0.67	—	0.45	—	0.58	—	0.92	—	0.56	—	0.22	—	0.68	—
2000 and later	0.79	-9.79***	0.81	-4.76***	0.83	-3.39***	0.33	2.63**	0.67	-1.28	0.64	-3.42***	0.79	-8.92***
By area where they stayed in the U.S.														
Not a large city	0.73	—	0.68	—	0.54	—	0.70	—	0.56	—	—	—	0.75	—
Large city	0.67	5.42***	0.78	-0.86	0.73	-2.28**	0.78	-0.37	0.73	-1.82*	—	—	0.66	6.56***

NOTE: — = not available. *significant at the 0.10 level (two-tailed test); **significant at the 0.05 level (two-tailed test); ***significant at the 0.01 level (two-tailed test). The hypothesis being tested is H_a: diff $\neq$ 0.

[a] Information on migrant residency while in the United States is not available in the Peruvian survey.

SOURCE: Author's tabulations using the MMP93 and the LAMP.

Table 5.4 Percentage of Income Remitted Home, by Documentation Status, Education, Decade, and City Dweller

Variable	All countries		Costa Rica		Dominican Republic		Haiti[a]		Nicaragua		Peru[b]		Mexico	
	%	t-stat.	%	t-stat.	%	t-stat.	%	t-stat.	%	t-stat.	%	t-stat.	%	t-stat.
By documentation status														
Legal	0.39	—	0.41	—	0.16	—	—	—	0.21	—	0.15	—	0.42	—
Unauthorized	0.41	-0.44	0.96	-1.34	0.17	-0.12	—	—	0.31	-0.65	0.22	—	0.41	0.40
By educational attainment														
Up to 15 years	0.20	—	0.14	—	0.13	—	—	—	0.10	—	0.19	—	0.23	—
16+ years	0.17	0.87	0.09	0.82	0.11	0.39	—	—	0.24	-1.41	0.06	1.75	0.18	1.07
By decade of visit														
During 1990s	0.30	—	0.28	—	0.09	—	—	—	0.14	—	0.03	—	0.31	—
2000 and later	0.28	0.83	0.46	-1.06	0.18	-2.02**	—	—	0.16	-0.36	0.13	-1.97*	0.28	1.34
By area where they stayed in the U.S.														
Not a large city	0.44	—	0.61	—	0.22	—	0.19	—	0.25	—	—	—	0.44	—
Large city	0.34	2.91***	0.22	1.28	0.14	1.29	0.11	1.75	0.17	0.83	—	—	0.36	2.34**

NOTE: — = not available. *significant at the 0.10 level (two-tailed test); **significant at the 0.05 level (two-tailed test); ***significant at the 0.01 level (two-tailed test). The hypothesis being tested is H_a: diff $\neq 0$.
[a] The limited number of observations for Haiti impedes a meaningful testing of statistically significant differences in most cases.
[b] Information on migrant residency while in the United States is not available in the Peruvian survey.
SOURCE: Author's tabulations using the MMP93 and the LAMP.

city while in the United States. Immigrants were more likely to remit (73 percent versus 67 percent, Table 5.3) and to remit a larger fraction of their monthly incomes (44 percent versus 34 percent, Table 5.4) if they resided in smaller cities or rural areas. When distinguishing by immigrants' country of origin, the same pattern is observed, partially as a result of the Mexican data being representative, to a large extent, of agricultural migrant workers. However, the percentage of migrants likely to remit in every country but Mexico (save Peru, where data are unavailable) is larger among those who last resided in a large U.S. city. This pattern may simply be indicative of the location preferences of some of these countries' emigrants: Dominicans may concentrate in New York City, for example.

Whereas Tables 5.3 and 5.4 cover the percentage of remitters and the magnitude of their remittance transfers by status, education, decade, and rurality, Tables 5.5 and 5.6 display how the same characteristics affect the purpose of funds remitted by immigrants. Perhaps the most noticeable result from Table 5.5 is that remitting for consumption purposes is not only more prominent among less educated immigrants than among more educated ones (43 versus 35 percent) but, in addition, it has become the predominant remitting motive among immigrants over the present decade (62 percent) as compared to the 1990s (43 percent). This overall trend holds true among immigrants from Costa Rica, the Dominican Republic, Peru, and Mexico, but not among those from Haiti and Nicaragua. Correspondingly, the data in Table 5.6 reveal how asset accumulation has lost importance over time in the overall sample. As a whole, asset accumulation appears to be a more prominent motive among legal immigrants than among unauthorized ones. Likewise, less educated Costa Ricans and Peruvians seem to cite asset accumulation as a reason for remitting money home on more occasions than their more educated counterparts. Finally, investment is more commonly a purpose for transferring funds by immigrants residing in large U.S. cities during their last trip, as is borne out by Costa Ricans and Mexicans.

In the following section, I take a look at households' reporting of these money inflows. I pay particular attention to the significance of remittances in the family budget as well as to how households make use of these money transfers.

Table 5.5 Percentage of Migrants Declaring Consumption as the Purpose for Remitting Money Home, by Documentation Status, Education, Decade, and City Dweller

Variable	All countries		Costa Rica		Dominican Republic		Haiti		Nicaragua		Peru[a]		Mexico	
	%	t-stat.	%	t-stat.	%	t-stat.	%	t-stat.	%	t-stat.	%	t-stat.	%	t-stat.
By documentation status														
Legal	0.78	—	0.84	—	0.89	—	0.82	—	0.84	—	0.73	—	0.77	—
Unauthorized	0.79	-0.78	0.86	-0.23	1.00	-3.33***	1.00	-1.49	0.88	-0.32	1.00	-2.81***	0.79	-1.49
By educational attainment														
Up to 15 years	0.43	—	0.39	—	0.57	—	0.35	—	0.42	—	0.32	—	0.42	—
16+ years	0.35	2.20**	0.33	0.32	0.64	-0.54	0.20	0.66	0.41	0.16	0.30	0.16	0.32	2.28***
By decade of visit														
During 1990s	0.43	—	0.20	—	0.34	—	0.12	—	0.27	—	0.06	—	0.46	—
2000 and later	0.62	-14.27***	0.65	-7.86***	0.72	-5.44***	0.09	0.37	0.06	-2.88***	0.48	-4.68***	0.63	-11.81***
By area where they stayed in the U.S.														
Not a large city	0.79	—	0.89	—	1.00	—	0.71	—	0.83	—	—	—	0.78	—
Large city	0.79	-0.02	0.50	4.00***	0.87	1.95***	1.00	-1.55	0.89	-0.69	—	—	0.79	-0.27

NOTE: — = not available. *significant at the 0.10 level (two-tailed test); **significant at the 0.05 level (two-tailed test); ***significant at the 0.01 level (two-tailed test). The hypothesis being tested is H_a: diff ≠ 0.

[a] Information on migrant residency while in the United States is not available in the Peruvian survey.

SOURCE: Author's tabulations using the MMP93 and the LAMP.

Table 5.6 Percentage of Migrants Declaring Asset Accumulation as the Purpose for Remitting Money Home, by Documentation Status, Education, Decade, and City Dweller

Variable	All countries		Costa Rica		Dominican Republic		Haiti		Nicaragua		Peru[a]		Mexico	
	%	t-stat.	%	t-stat.	%	t-stat.	%	t-stat.	%	t-stat.	%	t-stat.	%	t-stat.
By documentation status														
Legal	0.47	—	0.17	—	0.07	—	0.09	—	0.19	—	0.18	—	0.49	—
Unauthorized	0.43	2.12	0.11	0.91	0.00	2.73***	0.00	1.00	0.13	0.63	0.00	2.16**	0.48	0.94
By educational attainment														
Up to 15 years	0.19	—	0.15	—	0.09	—	0.09	—	0.11	—	0.11	—	0.23	—
16+ years	0.13	2.40**	0.00	3.23***	0.00	2.54***	0.00	1.45	0.05	1.02	0.05	0.76	0.21	0.63
By decade of visit														
During 1990s	0.29	—	0.05	—	0.03	—	0.01	—	0.06	—	0.02	—	0.33	—
2000 and later	0.24	4.44***	0.11	-1.66*	0.04	-0.16	0.00	1.00	0.04	-0.36	0.06	-0.85	0.27	4.29***
By area where they stayed in the U.S.														
Not a large city	0.43	—	0.11	—	0.00	—	0.14	—	0.15	—	—	—	0.45	—
Large city	0.50	-4.62***	0.50	-4.00***	0.09	-1.60	0.00	1.00	0.22	-0.79	—	—	0.53	-4.58***

NOTE: — = not available. *significant at the 0.10 level (two-tailed test); **significant at the 0.05 level (two-tailed test); ***significant at the 0.01 level (two-tailed test). The hypothesis being tested is H_a: diff $\neq$ 0.

[a] Information on migrant residency while in the United States is not available in the Peruvian survey.

SOURCE: Author's tabulations using the MMP93 and the LAMP.

HOUSEHOLD REMITTANCE RECEIPT AND ACTUAL USAGE

In addition to measuring remittance transfers and examining the motives behind immigrants' remitting patterns, the literature has long discussed how these money flows are used by migrants' families back home. This is of interest because immigrants' purposes for transferring money may not always coincide with the reported use of funds by the receiving families. In this regard, the MMP93 and LAMP ask households whether they receive any money transfers from abroad and whether these transfers represent a small, medium, or large portion of family income. Additionally, households are questioned about whether they use the reported funds for consumption or for asset accumulation purposes. Summary data of these findings are displayed in Figure 5.5 and Table 5.7.

Approximately 2 percent of the 21,263 households interviewed by the MMP93 and LAMP report receiving remittance transfers from abroad.[6] Table 5.7 displays slightly larger percentages of remittance-receiving households in Haiti (8 percent), the Dominican Republic (5 percent), and Costa Rica and Peru (both 3 percent) than in Nicaragua and Mexico (2 percent). Overall, 47 percent of the households reporting on the magnitude of remittance income declare that these funds constitute a large portion of household income (not shown). Separately, the various countries report similar percentages. The exception is Haitian households, most of whom declare these funds to be of medium size. Thus, dependence on remittance income may be a reality for some families in these Latin American and Caribbean nations.

Does the ultimate usage of remittance income by families coincide with the purpose for which immigrants transfer funds home? Figure 5.5 and the bottom category of Table 5.7 address the question of what remittances are used for. Thirty-eight percent of remittance-receiving households say they use remittance income for purchasing or adding to existing property (Figure 5.5). This percentage mirrors the 38 percent of immigrants declaring property investment as one of the motives for sending money back to their native country.[7] A comparable figure on the percentage of immigrants sending money back for consumption is, unfortunately, not available since households are only asked about the use of remittance income to purchase specific items, and only one

Figure 5.5 Types of Investment by Remittance-Receiving Households (%)

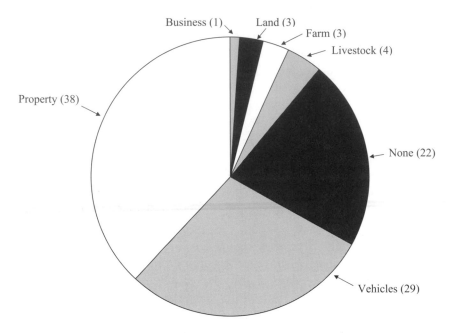

NOTE: Only 78 percent of households reported using remittances to purchase assets.
  The remaining 22 percent ("None") use remittances for consumption purposes.
SOURCE: Author's tabulations using the MMP93 and the LAMP.

of those items falls within the consumption category—vehicles, at 29
percent (Figure 5.5).

Large percentages of remittance-receiving households (Table 5.7)
declare using this income for asset accumulation purposes in Haiti (83
percent), Costa Rica (49 percent), the Dominican Republic (41 percent),
and Mexico (39 percent). Yet only in the case of Mexico is the percentage of receiving households declaring that they use remittances for asset accumulation approached by the percentage of immigrants declaring asset accumulation as one of the motives for sending money home,
as shown in Figure 5.4. In the other cases, households appear to be
using remittances to invest significantly more than is expected of them
by their remitting family members. Only 16 percent of Costa Rican
emigrants, 7 percent of Dominicans, and 7 percent of Haitians said they

Table 5.7 Proportion of Household Income Made Up by Remittances, and What Remittances Are Used For

Variable	Costa Rica		Dominican Republic		Haiti		Nicaragua		Peru		Mexico	
	N	%	N	%	N	%	N	%	N	%	N	%
% remittance-receiving households	39	0.03	51	0.05	30	0.08	40	0.02	19	0.03	264	0.02
% of households declaring remittances to be a small, medium, or large part of their income												
Small	36	0.28	51	0.27	30	0.13	39	0.28	19	0.26	264	0.40
Medium	36	0.19	51	0.22	30	0.60	39	0.21	19	0.16	264	0.13
Large	36	0.53	51	0.51	30	0.27	39	0.51	19	0.58	264	0.47
% of households declaring that they use remittances to finance consumption or asset accumulation												
Consumption (vehicles)[a]	39	0.26	51	0.33	30	0.53	40	0.15	19	0.26	264	0.28
Asset accumulation	39	0.49	51	0.41	30	0.83	40	0.13	19	0.32	264	0.39
Housing investments	39	0.41	51	0.37	30	0.80	40	0.13	19	0.32	264	0.37
Business	39	0.00	51	0.12	30	0.00	40	0.00	19	0.00	264	0.00
Land	39	0.10	51	0.00	30	0.00	40	0.03	19	0.00	264	0.04
Farm	39	0.13	51	0.02	30	0.00	40	0.03	19	0.00	264	0.03
Livestock	39	0.05	51	0.02	30	0.03	40	0.03	19	0.00	264	0.05

[a] The only specific form of consumption the survey asks about is the purchase of vehicles.

SOURCE: Author's tabulations using the MMP93 and the LAMP.

sent money home for asset accumulation purposes. This pattern is also observed among Peruvian households: 32 percent of remittance-receiving households in Peru use the remittances to purchase assets, whereas only 17 percent of Peruvian remitters report sending money home for asset accumulation purposes. In fact, only in Mexico and Nicaragua do households engage in less asset accumulation than is expected from remitters. In particular, 39 and 13 percent of Mexican and Nicaraguan remittance-receiving households report using remittance income to purchase assets, whereas 48 percent and 18 percent of Mexican and Nicaraguan remitters indicate investment as one of the purposes for transferring money home.

It is interesting to see how these funds are invested by country. In Costa Rica, as in most countries, remittance income is most often used to purchase housing investments (41 percent of remittance-receiving households indicate this usage). Thirteen and 10 percent of remittance-receiving Costa Rican households indicate farms and land, respectively, as secondary assets acquired with remittance income. In the Dominican Republic, the primary use of remittance income is also for housing stock acquisition (37 percent); however, for Dominicans business investments are the second use for the transferred funds (12 percent of households). In summary, the report from families does not support the notion that remittances do not serve investment purposes. Rather, it shows that a substantial percentage of households use the received money flows for asset accumulation purposes.

CONCLUSION

This study explores the similarities and differences in migration and remitting patterns of Latin Americans in the United States using data from two comparable survey instruments, the Mexican Migration Project (MMP93) and the Latin American Migration Project (LAMP).

The data reveal that 68 percent of Latin American immigrants in the sample—coming from Costa Rica, the Dominican Republic, Haiti, Nicaragua, Peru, and Mexico—are unauthorized. About 75 percent of these unauthorized immigrants rely on smuggling services to cross the border, paying $427 on average. While immigrants' reliance on smugglers and the money paid for such services vary across countries (depending, in part, on the country's proximity to the United States), smuggling costs have generally been on the rise for the past two decades. As such, it is not surprising to find that immigrants who use cheaper smuggling services cross the U.S. border more often than their counterparts who pay higher prices. Yet in some instances, such as with Costa Ricans and Nicaraguans, higher smuggling costs seem to be justified by a higher ratio of successful illegal border crossings.

About 70 percent of immigrants report that they remitted money back home on a monthly basis during their last U.S. trip. On average, migrants remitted $300 a month, or 40 percent of their earnings. These figures vary significantly across countries, with Dominicans sending an average of $179 a month, or 16 percent of their earnings, and Costa Ricans sending as much as $493 a month, or 55 percent of their earnings. When we examine immigrants' remitting motives, the data show that consumption is the most important motive for sending money home in the case of 79 percent of remitters. Consumption as the reason for remittance takes on greater importance for less educated immigrants or those who came to the United States in 2000 or later. However, a considerable proportion of immigrants (45 percent) report asset accumulation as one of their motives for transferring money to their families. Among Dominican, Haitian, Nicaraguan, and Costa Rican remitters, however, the importance of asset accumulation is significantly smaller, never surpassing 18 percent.

Examining households' remittance-receiving patterns and their usage of these money transfers, we see that about 45 percent of the 439 remittance-receiving households in the survey (2 percent of all households in the survey) report using these money transfers to purchase assets. As such, households appear to be investing remittances at a higher rate than is expected of them by their remitting family members. Most of the flows used for asset accumulation go toward acquiring property. Secondarily, 10 and 13 percent of remittance-receiving households in Costa Rica invest in land and farming, and 12 percent of such households in the Dominican Republic invest in business. In most instances, remittances constitute a significant portion of household income, meaning that these families rely to some extent on these flows.

The analysis reveals the different migration and remitting practices of Latin American emigrants as well as the diverse uses of remittance income by households, depending on the country. Given the mobility of workers and capital flows in Latin America and the Caribbean, it is important to gain a better understanding of these country-level differences and exploit them in the design of policies that maximize the economic potential of money flows in improving the livelihood of their recipients back home.

Notes

1. The Mexican Migration Project (MMP93) and the Latin American Migration Project (LAMP) are collaborative research projects based at Princeton University and the University of Guadalajara, supported by the National Institute of Child Health and Human Development (NICHD), Rockville, MD. The Web sites for MMP93 and LAMP can be found at http://mmp.opr.princeton.edu and http://lamp.opr.princeton.edu.

    The LAMP has also conducted research in Puerto Rico, Guatemala, and Paraguay. However, Guatemala and Paraguay were not included here because either the data sets were too small or (in the case of Paraguay) a modified version of the survey was used. Puerto Rico was omitted because of its link to the United States (whereby its migrants are all legal).

2. The MMP93 sample covers communities in the states of Aguascalientes, Baja California Norte, Chihuahua, Colima, Durango, Guanajuato, Guerrero, Hidalgo, Jalisco, Michoacán, Nayarit, Nuevo León, Oaxaca, Puebla, San Luis Potosí, Sinaloa, and Zacatecas.

3. The MMP93 interviews were conducted in communities of various size, ethnic composition, and economic development in typical source regions for U.S.-bound migrants. The sample has expanded over time to incorporate communities in newer sending states.

4. This figure of 6,392 includes the 5,837 immigrants from the MMP93 study, mentioned above, plus 555 immigrants from the LAMP.

5. These averages are for all countries in the study and are not represented in Figure 5.3.

6. This percentage, undoubtedly driven by the prominence of Mexican data in our joint sample, is close to the 5 percent of Mexican households who report receiving remittance transfers from abroad in the Encuesta Nacional de Ingresos y Gastos de los Hogares (ENIGH). The ENIGH is a representative Mexican household survey of income and expenditures carried out by the INEGI—the Instituto Nacional de Estadistica, Geografia, e Informática, or the Mexican National Institute of Statistics, Geography and Information (Amuedo-Dorantes and Pozo 2005).

7. The 38 percent figure represents the aggregation of the country-level averages shown in Figure 5.4.

References

Amuedo-Dorantes, Catalina, Cynthia Bansak, and Susan Pozo. 2005. "On the Remitting Pattern of Immigrants: Evidence from Mexican Survey Data." *Economic Review* 90(1): 37–58.

Amuedo-Dorantes, Catalina, and Susan Pozo. 2005. "Remittances and the Healthcare Use of Populations in Origin Communities: Evidence from Mexico." Paper presented at the 2005 Midwest Economics Association meeting, held in Milwaukee, WI, March 11–13; and at the 2005 Population Association of America meeting, held in Philadelphia, PA, March 31–April 2.

———. 2006. "Remittances as Insurance: Evidence from Mexican Immigrants." *Journal of Population Economics* 19(2): 227–254.

Bauer, Thomas, and Mathias Sinning. 2005. "The Savings Behaviour of Temporary and Permanent Migrants in Germany." CEPR Discussion Paper 5102. London: Centre for Economic Policy Research.

Becker, Gary S. 1974. "A Theory of Social Interactions." *Journal of Political Economy* 82(6): 1063–1093.

Cox, Donald. 1987. "Motives for Private Transfers." *Journal of Political Economy* 95(3): 508–546.

de la Garza, Rodolfo O., and Briant Lindsay Lowell. 2002. *Sending Money Home: Hispanic Remittances and Community Development*. Lanham, MD: Rowman and Littlefield.

de Vasconcelos, Pedro. 2004. "Sending Money Home: Remittances to Latin America from the United States." http://www.iadb.org/publications/search.cfm?language=English&topics=CM-REM (accessed January 2, 2007).

Ilahi, Nadeem, and Saqib Jafarey. 1999. "Guestworker Migration, Remittances and the Extended Family: Evidence from Pakistan." *Journal of Development Economics* 58(2): 485–512.

Lucas, Robert E.B., and Oded Stark. 1985. "Motivations to Remit: Evidence from Botswana." *Journal of Political Economy* 93(5): 901–918.

Massey, Douglas S., and René Zenteno. 2000. "A Validation of the Ethnosurvey: The Case of Mexico-U.S. Migration." *International Migration Review* 34(3): 766–793.

Munshi, Kaivan. 2003. "Networks in the Modern Economy: Mexican Migrants in the U.S. Labor Market." *Quarterly Journal of Economics* 118(2): 549–599.

Taylor, J. Edward. 1999. "The New Economics of Labour Migration and the Role of Remittances in the Migration Process." *International Migration* 37(1): 63–88.

6
Remittances in the Pacific

David J. McKenzie
Development Research Group, The World Bank

Small island states have among the highest rates of migration in the world (Table 6.1).[1] The average island country with a population of under 1.5 million has 17 percent of all its citizens living overseas, and several of these island nations have more than 30 percent of their citizens abroad. Many of the Pacific Islands follow this pattern; for instance, approximately one-third of Samoa's and Tonga's populations live in another country. Some of the smallest islands in the Pacific have even more dramatic migration rates: more individuals born in Niue and Tokelau now live in New Zealand than on either of these two islands.[2] Together with high migration rates one finds heavy dependence on ro mittances in many of these countries.[3] For the year 2004, Tonga, the main subject of this chapter, had remittances equal to 39 percent of GDP, the highest measured rate in the world.

The growing size of remittances around the world has led researchers to give renewed attention to their importance for development and has prompted officials to engage in discussion of policies designed to increase the benefits of migration (Global Commission on International Migration 2005; World Bank 2005). One question that can arise in these discussions is whether there is scope for countries such as Tonga, which already receives large remittance flows, to further increase the benefits from remittances. This chapter will use a recently conducted survey of Tongan migrants in New Zealand, and of Tongans in Tonga, to argue that there is still a sizable scope for policies designed to lower the costs of sending money and improve the knowledge of migrants and their families about remittance products.

The survey I use here collects much more detailed information on remittance transactions than is commonly the case. I use this information to provide a description of some aspects of remittances that are typically missed in standard surveys; these additional aspects have im-

Table 6.1 Migration and Remittance Rates for Small Islands

	Population (000s)	% migrants	Remittances (% GDP)	Main destination
Africa				
Cape Verde	470	18.7	11.5	Portugal
Comoros	600	3.2	3.8	France
Mauritius	1,222	6.9	4.0	France
Sao Tome and Principe	157	8.5	1.7	Portugal
Seychelles	84	8.7	0.3	United Kingdom
Caribbean				
Antigua and Barbuda	79	28.9	1.5	United States
Dominica	71	32.0	1.6	United States
Grenada	195	23.8	5.3	United States
St. Kitts and Nevis	47	38.5	1.1	United States
St. Lucia	161	17.5	0.6	United States
St. Vincent and Grenadines	109	31.1	0.8	United States
Trinidad and Tobago	1,313	18.8	0.8	United States
Pacific Islands				
Fiji	835	13.5	1.1	Australia
Kiribati	96	2.4	12.0	United States
Marshall Islands	53	13.0	—	United States
Micronesia, Federated States of	125	12.2	—	United States
Palau	20	20.2	—	United States
Samoa	178	35.1	14.2	New Zealand
Solomon Islands	457	0.5	0.9	Australia
Tonga	102	31.1	39.2	New Zealand
Vanuatu	210	1.0	3.3	Australia
South Asia				
Maldives	293	0.8	0.4	India

NOTE: — = data not available.
SOURCE: Remittances and population from World Development Indicators central database (August 2005 update); migration stocks and destinations from foreign-born Version 4 of the Global Trade Analysis Project (GTAP) database in Parsons et al. (2005).

plications for the measurement of remittances. The survey also matches a small sample of migrants in New Zealand to their family members remaining in Tonga, and both groups are interviewed. I conclude by using this matched sample to look at how expectations for the continuation of remittances differ between migrants and their families.

A BRIEF HISTORY OF TONGAN MIGRATION TO NEW ZEALAND

The Kingdom of Tonga is an archipelago of islands in the South Pacific, about two-thirds of the way from Hawaii to New Zealand.[4] The population is just over 100,000, and more than 30,000 additional Tongans live abroad (Table 6.1). Tongan migration to New Zealand really began in the 1960s and 1970s, when Tongans began arriving on temporary permits to take up work opportunities. After their permits expired, some returned to Tonga and others stayed on in New Zealand illegally. An amnesty in 1976 granted many of these illegals permanent residence.

Migration for work continued in the late 1970s and into the 1980s, and by 1986 the Tongan population in New Zealand had reached 13,600. In 1991 New Zealand introduced a points-based selection system for immigration, in which potential migrants are awarded points for education, skills, and business capital. Few Tongans qualified to migrate under this points system, so most Tongan migration during the 1990s was under family-sponsored categories—as the spouse, parent, or child of an existing migrant. For example, in fiscal year 1998, only 29 Tongans were admitted as principal applicants under the points system, compared to 436 under family categories. With family migration, the Tongan-born population in New Zealand had grown to 19,000 by the 2001 census.

In early 2002 another channel was opened up for immigration to New Zealand, through the creation of the Pacific Access Category (PAC), which allows for a quota of 250 Tongans to emigrate to New Zealand each year. Applicants in this category must be between the ages of 18 and 45, meet requirements for health, character, and a minimum level of English-speaking ability, and have an offer of employment in

New Zealand. It is the group of new migrants in this category that I shall discuss.

DATA

The main source of data I use is the Tongan component of the Pacific Island–New Zealand Migration Survey (PINZMS), conducted in the first half of 2005. The PINZMS uses a sample frame of applicants in the Pacific Access Category. More individuals apply to migrate than the quota allows, so a lottery is used to allocate visas among applicants. A comparison of winners and losers in this lottery is a feature of other works that use this survey to estimate the causal effect of migration on a number of migration outcomes (McKenzie, Gibson, and Stillman 2006; Stillman, McKenzie, and Gibson 2006). In addition to sampling migrants in New Zealand who come through the PAC, the survey includes a sample of applicants for the quota who remain in Tonga, a sample of nonapplicants who live in the same villages as the applicants, and a sample of remaining household members of the migrants in New Zealand. The first round provides a sample of 65 migrant households in New Zealand and 230 households in Tonga. Forty-five out of the 65 migrants in New Zealand left behind household members in Tonga, and we were able to survey 28 of these remaining households.

The PINZMS is a multitopic, detailed survey designed to look at many aspects of the migration process. Detailed modules on remittances are given to migrant households in New Zealand and to all households in Tonga. The survey collects information on remittances sent and received by both groups, separates these into money and goods flows, collects information on the channels used to send remittances, and asks a number of questions about knowledge of remittance methods and expectations of future remittance patterns.[5]

I supplement the PINZMS survey with information on the cost of sending remittances, gathered directly from remittance service providers. For this chapter, for comparison purposes, I have additionally collected information on the costs of sending from Australia to several Pacific Island countries, and from the United States to a couple of small Caribbean countries.[6]

THE HIGH COST OF REMITTING IN THE PACIFIC

There are two main financial costs involved in sending money across borders.[7] The first is the fee charged by the remittance-sending company, which is usually fixed or a step function. For example, ANZ and Westpac banks in New Zealand charge a fixed fee of NZ$25 to send a telegraphic transfer (wire transfer) from a bank account in New Zealand to a bank account in Tonga. Western Union charges a fixed fee of NZ$20 in New Zealand to send to Tonga or Samoa, but it charges a stepped fee in Australia: A$15 for amounts of A$75 or less, A$20 for amounts of A$76–$300, and A$25 for amounts of A$301–$999.

This component of the cost is the one most easily seen by consumers. However, the second component of the cost is less transparent. In addition to the fixed fee, remittance-sending companies typically make money by offering migrants a less advantageous exchange rate than the interbank rate. The exchange rate commission charged by the bank or remittance-sending company can be calculated by the equation

$$(6.1) \quad R = \frac{100 \times (Interbank\ Rate - Offered\ Rate)}{Interbank\ Rate}.$$

For example, at the interbank rate,[8] NZ$100 would buy 138.71 pa'anga. However, at the exchange rate offered by ANZ Bank, one would instead receive 135.79 pa'anga (and also have to pay the fixed fee). The exchange rate commission of 2.1 percent therefore represents a loss of pa'anga compared to what one would receive at the interbank rate. Figure 6.1 graphs the exchange rate commission from New Zealand and Australia to a number of different Pacific Island countries for ANZ Bank telegraphic transfers and Western Union transactions. For comparison purposes I also show rates from Australia to the United States and New Zealand, and the Western Union rate from the United States to Mexico, one of the world's most competitive markets.

The figure shows a wide range of exchange rate commissions, from just over 1 percent to nearly 12. The highest commission is charged by Melie mei Langi, a church-run remittance channel for sending money from New Zealand to Tonga. This channel charges an extremely low fixed fee (NZ$5), which is attractive to those who send small amounts,

Figure 6.1 Exchange Rate Commission on Remittances

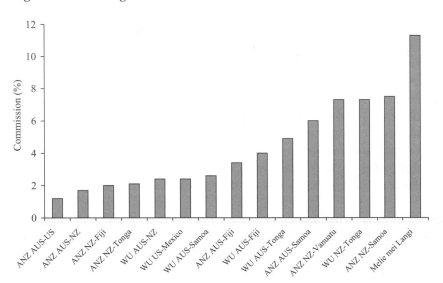

NOTE: ANZ = ANZ Bank Telegraphic Transfer rate; WU = Western Union rate;
  AUS = Australia; NZ = New Zealand; US = United States.
SOURCE: Author's calculations from supplementary data collected on remittance
  costs.

even though they must pay a high exchange rate commission. Moreover, even between ANZ Bank and Western Union, it is not the case that one company always offers the better rate: Western Union has a lower rate to Samoa but higher rates to Tonga, for example.

Figure 6.2 plots the overall cost of remitting from New Zealand to Tonga by different channels, expressing the cost as a percentage of the amount remitted. The cheapest method by far is to use an ATM card: migrants in New Zealand can give their relative a second card, which can then be used to withdraw cash from the ATM for a fee of NZ$5–$8 for most banks. The other methods all have much higher fixed fees, resulting in extremely high costs for remitting small amounts. For example, remitting NZ$100 (US$68) ends up costing 25–30 percent of the amount remitted.

These high levels of costs are not atypical in the Pacific and are higher than in many other regions of the world. Figure 6.3 shows that the cost of sending from New Zealand to Tonga is very similar to that

**Figure 6.2 Remittance Costs from New Zealand to Tonga by
Various Means**

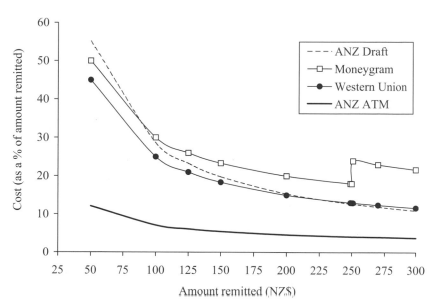

SOURCE: Adapted from Gibson, McKenzie, and Rohorua (2006).

of sending from Australia to other Pacific Island countries, and is higher
than sending from the United States to Mexico, and from the United
States to Grenada, another small island country. In Gibson, McKenzie,
and Rohorua (2006), we compare the cost of sending US$200 (NZ$294)
by way of different remittance channels around the world. The cost of
15–23 percent from New Zealand to Tonga is approximately twice the
average cost of sending from France, Germany, the United States or the
United Kingdom to a wide variety of destinations, including Pakistan,
Mozambique, Portugal, Greece, and the Philippines. This is not simply
a result of small economies of scale in Tonga, since Ghana and Mozambique, which receive the same total volume of remittances as Tonga,
have costs of 5 percent or less for sending this amount.

These high costs of sending money in the Pacific therefore suggest that there is room for policies aimed at lowering these costs. The
question that then arises is how sensitive remittance senders are to the
cost. We asked Tongan migrants in New Zealand how much they sent

Figure 6.3 Comparison of Remittance Costs in the Pacific to those from the United States

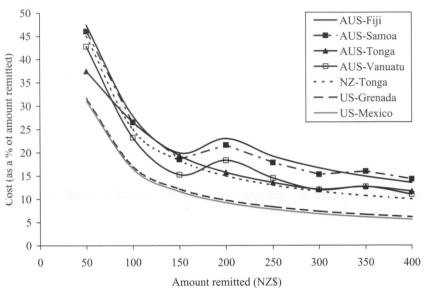

NOTE: Amounts shown are based on Western Union rates from Australia and Money-gram rates from the United States.
SOURCE: Author's calculations from supplementary data collected on remittance costs.

in their last remittance transaction, the cost of sending this, and how much they would have sent if fees had been only half as much. Based on these answers, Gibson, McKenzie, and Rohorua (2006) estimate that the average cost-elasticity of remittances is −0.22, so that when costs fall, remitters will send more remittances. As an example, if the cost of sending from New Zealand to Tonga were to fall to levels just above those between the United States and Mexico, we calculate that instead of sending NZ$200, remitters would send NZ$228, and receiving households would experience a 27.5 percent increase in the amount of remittances received in local currency.[9] Given the large share remittances already make up in household incomes, this is a sizable potential gain.

WHAT CAN BE DONE TO REDUCE COSTS?

These high costs therefore do suggest that there is scope for increasing remittances, even in a country like Tonga, which already receives a large amount. What, then, can be done to reduce remittance costs? The World Bank's (2005) recent *Global Economic Prospects 2006* report on remittances emphasizes three policies for lowering remittance transaction costs:

1) Promoting competition,

2) Improving access of migrants to the financial system, and

3) Disseminating information.

In the case of the Pacific, migrants do have a range of options available for sending money. The small size of these economies suggests that there is likely to be a limit on the number of separate banks and money transfer operators that can offer services. I therefore do not think there is much scope for enhancing competition through further entry of new remittance providers. All of the Tongan migrants we surveyed in New Zealand who send remittances have bank accounts, and 98 percent have ATM cards. Among the sample of households in Tonga, 79 percent have bank accounts and 54 percent have ATM cards. ANZ and Westpac banks both have four ATM locations in Tonga, and Western Union has 18 locations. There is thus some scope for expansion of access to financial services within Tonga, which would make it easier for migrants' family members to receive remittances through direct bank transfers and ATMs. As we saw, the ATM card transaction has by far the lowest fee, so any expansion of this channel can potentially have a large effect on reducing costs.

What would be the effect of information dissemination? The pricing of remittance transactions is rather opaque, particularly with regard to the exchange rate component. Phone calls to several of the nonbank remittance-sending companies were met with suspicion and, in some cases, refusal to provide information on the exchange rate or cost of sending without our visiting the office in person. Moreover, many migrants are not aware of the size of the commission being charged, or of what the interbank exchange rate actually is. We asked migrants in New Zealand and remittance receivers in Tonga what the New Zealand-to-Tonga exchange rate was. Figure 6.4 shows a histogram of the answers from those in Tonga; the dual vertical lines show the Westpac/ANZ exchange rate (left line) and the Interbank exchange rate (right line). Although the exchange rate was stable over the survey period, the mean and median exchange rate quoted by the Tongan remittance receivers both missed the mark widely—they are around 120 pa'anga per NZ$100, which understates the true exchange rate (136 pa'anga per NZ$100) by about 12 percent. Similarly, among migrants sending remittances, the mean reported exchange rate was 122 pa'anga per NZ$100. Therefore, Tongans displayed a wide lack of knowledge about the exchange rate whether they were sending or receiving remittances—thus affording remittance companies an opportunity to extract high commissions.

In addition to possessing incomplete information about the exchange rate, many remittance senders and receivers have a limited knowledge about the variety of different remittance-sending methods that are available. The PINZMS survey asked senders and receivers whether they knew about particular methods and whether they had used them. Table

Figure 6.4 Tongans' Estimates of the New Zealand–Tonga Exchange Rate (pa'anga per NZ$100)

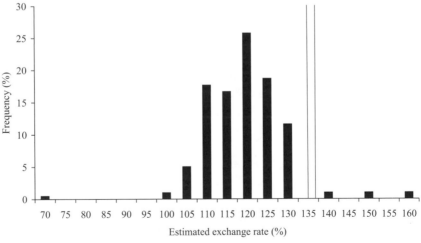

NOTE: Left line marks the Westpac/ANZ exchange rate; right line shows where the Interbank exchange rate falls.
SOURCE: Author's calculations from PINZMS (2007) data.

6.2 shows that almost all remitters and remittees know about Western Union and most have used it. Only about half of the remitters in New Zealand know how to send bank transfers by means of various banks, and much fewer than half actually do so. Melie mei Langi is known and used by about half the migrants but is less well known among the receivers, who know more about Moneygram.[10] Despite ATMs being the cheapest method, only 2 percent know about sending money this way. None of the respondents knew about iKobo.com, a low-cost Internet-based method for sending money.

Table 6.2 Knowledge and Use of Different Remittance Channels (%)

Channel	Remittance senders in New Zealand		Remittance receivers in Tonga	
	Know	Use	Know	Use
Friend or relative paying for airfare		6.8		2.9
Friend or relative bringing back money on visit		4.5		4.9
Sending/receiving money through family/friends visiting overseas		13.6		4.4
Sending/receiving money through another person		45.5		28.6
Sending/receiving money through my church	9.1	2.3	1.5	0.5
Traveler's check	2.3	0.0	1.5	0.5
Bank transfer through ANZ	47.7	0.0	13.1	5.3
Bank transfer through Westpac	52.3	4.5	13.1	4.9
Bank transfer through another bank	38.6	2.3	8.7	1.5
Western Union	95.5	77.3	92.2	90.3
Travelex	6.8	6.8	1.5	1.0
Moneygram	6.8	2.3	46.6	43.7
Melie mei Langi	47.7	47.7	24.8	24.8
iKobo.com	0.0	0.0	0.0	0.0
ATM card or credit card from relative	2.3	2.3	2.4	1.0
Sample size	49	49	206	206

NOTE: Knowledge of the first four categories was assumed.
SOURCE: PINZMS (2007).

Thus, while competition does exist, and while migrants and their families generally do have access to bank accounts, the ability of both of these factors to help lower remittance costs seems to be hampered by a lack of information. There appears to be a role for information dissemination in increasing the benefits of competition and allowing migrants to obtain lower costs. The relatively small size of migrant communities may act as a barrier to widespread advertising campaigns by money transfer companies, and the time involved in researching their options may make it hard for individual migrants to know whether or not they are getting a good deal. This then suggests a role for community organizations or migrant news organizations, which could better disseminate this information.[11] Weekly newspapers that have as their audience the Fijian, Tongan, and Samoan communities in New Zealand could provide a listing of the fixed-cost exchange rate premium and the amounts received from sending $NZ100 and $NZ200 by way of different mechanisms.

WHAT DOES A RICHER REMITTANCE SURVEY TELL US ABOUT REMITTANCES?

The second part of this chapter involves dimensions of remittances that standard surveys and official statistics may not pick up very well. Standard household income and expenditure surveys typically ask for little detailed information about remittances. For example, the ENIGH surveys in Mexico only report the annual value of remittances received by households.[12] Even more specialized migration surveys such as the Mexican Migration Project (MMP93) and the Latin American Migration Project (LAMP) only ask respondents for the average monthly remittances sent and the purpose of these remittances.[13] In contrast, the PINZMS has 10 pages of questions on remittances and thus is able to provide richer detail on some important aspects of remittance transactions.

The first aspect of the various dimensions of remittance surveys that I consider is what is being measured by remittances. Officially recorded remittances form a large share of GDP in many Pacific countries, but they do not capture all of the remittance action occurring. First, as

Figure 6.5   Ratio of Price of Durable Goods in Tonga to Price in New Zealand

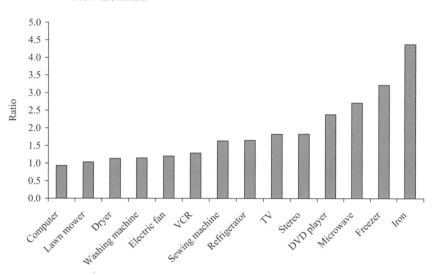

SOURCE: Prices collected in New Zealand and Tonga in September 2005 for the PINZMS (2007) data set.

seen in Table 6.2, a number of remittance transactions occur through informal channels, such as sending money back with friends or family visiting from overseas. Second, in addition to cash, migrants also remit goods such as consumer durables. These can be particularly important in small island economies where the supply of durable goods is limited and prices are higher than in the migrant destinations. For the sample of 14 durable goods shown in Figure 6.5, the price in Tonga averages 1.7 times the price in New Zealand.

The PINZMS asked migrants separately about the remittances they had sent as monetary transfers and the remittances sent in the form of goods. On average, cash remittances accounted for 75 percent of total remittances sent and 63 percent of total remittances received by all remittance receivers in Tonga (not just those receiving from the New Zealand sample). Therefore surveys and official statistics that focus solely on monetary transfers in the Pacific Islands are likely to miss 25–40 percent of remittance transactions. Goods remittances are also important in other areas of the world, although more work elsewhere is needed to generalize this result to obtain an estimate of the undercount of remittances at a world level.

Another understudied aspect of remittance transactions is reverse flows. Migrants not only send cash and goods to family members back home but also receive them from home. Twenty-two percent of the migrants who had sent remittances from New Zealand to Tonga had also received remittances from Tonga. However, remittances received are mostly in the form of goods rather than cash—on average, cash received by migrants accounts for only 11 percent of the total remittances they receive, whereas goods account for 89 percent. These goods often tend to be handicrafts, food, and other goods that carry nostalgic value. On average these goods equal 43 percent of the value of remittances sent by the migrants in New Zealand, meaning that the net flow of remittances is substantially smaller than the gross flow.[14]

The next aspect that a richer survey reveals is that many remittances do not come from former household members. Figure 6.6 uses the sample of remittance receivers in Tonga to plot the share of remittances received according to the sender's relationship to the household head. Both value shares and frequency shares are shown, in case one or two very rich relatives are driving all of the value share results. Remittances received by former household members who moved to New Zealand through the Pacific Access Category (that is, PAC household members) are the only remittances that we know for sure came from a former household member. Spouses abroad are also almost certain to be former household members, while children would have been household members at some stage but may have been living outside of the household before migration. These three groups, however, together account for only 34 percent of the value of remittances received and 21 percent of the number of remittance transactions.

Parents of the head and spouse of the head may or may not have lived with the household before migration. Siblings of the household head are much more likely to send remittances than siblings of the spouse of the head. However, it is likely that many of these brothers and sisters of the head were not living in the household before migration. The largest source of remittances is other relatives, such as cousins, uncles, aunts, grandparents, and other extended family. This shows that the benefits of a single individual migrating spread beyond the household he or she was living in at the time, and that the extended family benefits from

Figure 6.6 Sources from Whom Tongans Receive Remittances

Value Shares (%)

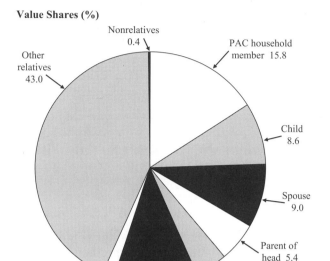

Nonrelatives 0.4

PAC household member 15.8

Other relatives 43.0

Child 8.6

Spouse 9.0

Parent of head 5.4

Parent of spouse 4.7

Sibling of head 11.0

Sibling of spouse 1.5

Frequency Shares (%)

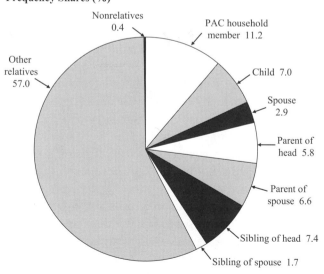

Nonrelatives 0.4

PAC household member 11.2

Other relatives 57.0

Child 7.0

Spouse 2.9

Parent of head 5.8

Parent of spouse 6.6

Sibling of head 7.4

Sibling of spouse 1.7

NOTE: Percentages in top chart do not add up to 100 percent because of rounding. In the bottom chart, the term "Frequency Shares" refers to the share of the number of transactions contributed by each category of remitter.

SOURCE: PINZMS (2007).

these remittances as well. The mean remitter sends remittances to 1.25 distinct groups of people, and the mean remittance-receiving household in Tonga receives remittances from 1.22 people. However, these means are the result of a few individuals sending or receiving remittances to or from three people—the median remitter only sends remittances to one person, and the median remittee only receives remittances from one person, just not necessarily a former household member.

WHY MIGHT REMITTANCES BE SPENT DIFFERENTLY FROM OTHER FORMS OF INCOME?

The development impact of remittances depends on their sustainability and what remittances are spent on. Many studies have looked to see if remittances are spent differently from other sources of income. One reason remittances might be spent differently is that migrants send remittances in response to specific events, or conditional on certain actions being taken. Remittance receivers in Tonga reported that 66 percent of all remittance transactions received were earmarked for a special purpose. The main purposes were the *misinale* (a once-a-year gift made to the church [Puloka 2003]), which accounted for 33 percent of special purpose remittances, 28 percent of payment of school fees, and 14 percent of funeral expenses. Remittances received for funeral expenses can be considered a form of insurance, and therefore will be spent differently than an increase in general household income. Remittances sent for other special purposes will only alter spending patterns compared to the same increase in household income if the conditions placed on them are binding, or if the fact that they are received as remittances increases the cost of certain expenses. This might be the case for misinale payments and schooling, if families receiving remittances are expected to pay more.[15]

A second reason remittances may be spent differently than other sources of income is that households view them as being more temporary in nature. Standard economic theory suggests that households will save a larger fraction of transitory income (or invest it in schooling and housing) than they would for permanent income. However, the cross-sectional nature of existing remittance surveys provides us with little

Table 6.3 Mean Expected Chance Of Remitting/Receiving Remittances

	Migrants	Remaining household
In 1 year's time	79.6	78.1
In 5 years' time	63.7	68.3
In 10 years' time	31.5	36.9

SOURCE: PINZMS (2007).

information on how households expect remittances to vary over time, and whether these expectations match those of the migrants.

Our survey asked migrants what they thought the percent chance was that they would remit in 1 year's time if they were still in New Zealand. This was followed by similar questions for 5 and 10 years' time. Similarly, the head of the household that the migrant had been a part of was asked what he or she thought was the percent chance that the migrant would remit in 1, 5, and 10 years' time if the migrant was still in New Zealand. We were able to match 28 migrants to their remaining family members. Table 6.3 shows the average percent chance reported for different periods. On average, migrants and their families have very similar expectations: both have high expectations of remittances occurring 1 year out, but lower expectations of remittances occurring in 5 and 10 years. That is, many remittance receivers believe that remittances will be a short-term source of income.

Not only does the average expectation of receiving remittances decline over time, but the expectation declines for almost every single family. Figure 6.7 shows that families with higher expectations of receiving remittances in 1 year also have higher expectations of receiving remittances in 5 and 10 years, but that the percent chance of receiving is almost always less than the 1-year-out expectation.

However, although on average migrants and their families have similar expectations, when we look at the matched pairs, a very different pattern arises. Figure 6.8 shows the match between migrant and family expectations for remittances in 1 year and in 10 years. There is a much looser relationship for expectations 1 year out than 10 years out: the rank-order correlation is 0.27 for 1 year (insignificantly different from zero) and 0.43 for 10 years (significantly different from zero at the 0.05 level). At 1 year out, there is a group of migrants who have very

Figure 6.7 Expectations of Receiving Remittances Decay over Time

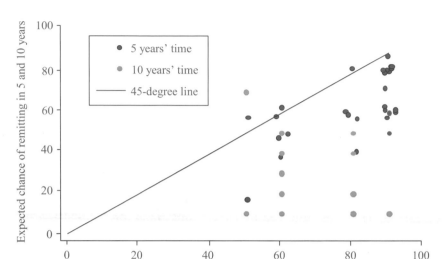

NOTE: The data consist of pairs of expectations, where an x,y pairing of (1-year expectation, 5-year expectation) is represented by one set of dots, and an x,y pairing of
(1-year expectation, 10-year expectation) is represented by another set of dots. The
45-degree line shows what the 5- and 10-year expectations would be if they were the
same as the 1-year expectations.
SOURCE: PINZMS (2007).

high expectations of remitting, but whose families have low expectations of receiving remittances, and another group whose families expect
remittances, but who don't expect to be sending them.

This difference between the remittance expectations of migrants
and their families 1 year out may reflect uncertainty over how long it
will take the migrant to get settled in his new country and start earning sufficient income to send remittances. Regression of the difference
between the family's expectations and the migrant's expectations on
characteristics of the migrant finds the family to have higher expectations than the migrant when the migrant is currently unemployed, and
when the migrant states there is a high probability of losing his job in
the next year and a low probability of being employed in 1 year's time.
However, these correlates are only suggestive; as with the small sample

Figure 6.8 Relationship between Migrant and Family Expectations for Remittances in 1 Year, 10 Years

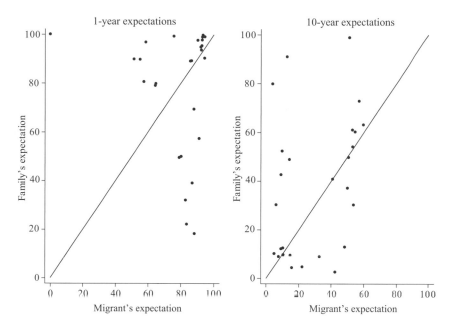

SOURCE: PINZMS (2007).

size of matched observations, no explanatory variables were significant in the regression.[16] In contrast, expectations are much more aligned 10 years out—this is sufficiently long enough for migrants to have become established and to have found a good job.

Note that both migrants and their families have lower expectations of remittances being sent in 10 years' time than they do in one year's time. This decay in the probability of sending remittances suggests that remittances are viewed as a transitory form of income, which suggests that receiving households should save or invest a higher proportion of the income received from remittances than they would from a wage income that was higher by the same amount. Nevertheless, this does not necessarily mean that the level of remittances received by Tonga from this group of Tongan migrants will decay over time—it may be the case that falling probabilities of remitting are accompanied by higher amounts sent when remittances actually do occur. Most existing studies of remittance decay are cross-sectional in nature and thus not able to capture these dynamic aspects.[17]

CONCLUSION

Migration and remittances are of large importance to a number of Pacific Island nations. This chapter has attempted to show that even though these countries currently receive a lot of remittances, there is still scope for further remittance growth, because the high costs of sending money may discourage some remittance. Expansion of ATM services and provision of information on exchange rate commissions and the remittance options available seem promising avenues for lowering these costs.

I have also highlighted some aspects of remittances that may not so easily be seen in traditional surveys. Remittances occur as goods as well as cash, are often accompanied by sizable reverse flows, and, at least in the case of the Pacific Islands, are sent to the extended family in addition to direct household members. Matching migrants to their remaining household members shows that both groups expect the likelihood of remittances occurring to decrease with the time spent overseas, and that there is more concurrence in expectations in the long term than in the short term. These findings are drawn from a rather small sample of matched migrants, and so in future research it will be useful to see whether they hold for larger samples and for migrants from other countries.

Notes

This chapter builds on surveys and joint work conducted with John Gibson and Halahingano Rohorua. Thanks to John Gibson for useful comments.

1. Measurement of migration stocks and remittances received is poor in a number of countries, so the numbers in Table 6.1 should be treated with caution.
2. The population of Niue is 1,761, yet 5,328 Niue-born citizens live in New Zealand; Tokelau's population is 1,513, yet 1,662 Tokelau-born citizens live in New

Zealand. These figures are according to the Government of Niue (2004) and Statistics New Zealand (2001a,b).

3. Connell and Brown (2005) provide a recent overview of remittances in Pacific Island countries and discuss reasons why some of the relatively high-migration islands receive small remittances.

4. This section is based on information from *The World Factbook* (CIA 2006) and from *Te Ara: The Encyclopedia of New Zealand* (Taumoefolau 2006).

5. The PINZMS data come from a survey conducted by the author. A Web site dedicated to reporting the findings of this survey is at http://www.pacificmigration .ac.nz.

6. Costs of sending from New Zealand to Tonga were collected in March 2005, at the time of the PINZMS survey (see Gibson, McKenzie, and Rohorua [2006] for details). Costs of sending from Australia and the United States via Western Union and Moneygram were collected in January 2006.

7. A third potential cost faced by the receiver is a charge for receiving remittances. For example, Westpac Bank in Tonga charges a fee to receive a telegraphic transfer or deposit a bank draft. Western Union typically does not charge the recipient, although there may be a fee to notify the recipient if he or she is in a distant location. A fourth cost that occurs in some areas of the world is the "float" or overnight interest collected by remittance companies (World Bank 2005). This is not a major element in the Pacific.

8. As obtained from http://www.oanda.com. The interbank rate is the market rate used between banks for transactions of US$1 million or more. This is the "official rate" typically quoted in the media.

9. The percentage increase in remittances received in local currency is the combination of two factors: 1) for each New Zealand dollar of remittances sent, a reduction in remittance costs leads to more Tongan pa'anga being received, and 2) senders in New Zealand also will send more New Zealand dollars when remittance costs fall. The 27.5 percent increase in local currency is the combination of these two factors.

10. Note that the sample of receivers includes those receiving money from family members who have migrated to New Zealand, Australia, and the United States through other methods than the Pacific Access Category, the category that the sample of migrants come from.

11. An alternative would be for the Pacific Island consulates to provide this service for their migrants. Mexico's consulates in the United States collect weekly data on the costs of sending money from nine cities in the United States and publish it on Mexico's consumer protection Web site, http://www.profeco.gob.mx.

12. ENIGH stands for Encuesta Nacional de Ingreso y Gasto de los Hogares, or the National Survey of Household Incomes and Expenses.

13. See Amuedo-Dorantes (2005) and documentation on the MMP93 and LAMP Web pages, found at http://mmp.opr.princeton.edu and http://lamp.opr.princeton.edu, respectively. The questionnaires are contained at http://mmp.opr.princeton.edu/ databases/ethnosurvey-en.aspx and http://lamp.opr.princeton.edu/documents-en .aspx.

14. This pattern of bidirectional remittance flows involving goods as well as cash corresponds to findings of other remittance studies in the Pacific. See Connell and Brown (2005) for a review.

15. This may be because families with migrants are expected to contribute more to local public goods since having a migrant member is seen as a source of wealth, as well as because migrant members planning on returning may be expected to contribute to local public goods while away, so that the family merely acts as an intermediary between the migrant and the community.

16. I also tried regressing the difference and the absolute difference in expectations on age, education, sex, marital status, past income in Tonga, current income in New Zealand, the difference in income, and the difference in employment status. These variables were tried one by one, and also in groups. Current unemployment had the largest economic effect (associated with a 23 percent gap in expectations) and the highest t-statistic (1.4) in this regression.

17. Connell and Brown (2005) survey several studies of remittance decay in the Pacific and conclude there is little statistically significant evidence for remittance decay. There are two main concerns with many of these cross-sectional studies. The first is that they may rely on community networks to obtain a sample of migrants, so that only migrants who remain tied to their communities (and hence more likely to continue remitting) appear in the sample. If more recent migrants are more likely to rely on membership of these ethnic networks, this will result in a systematic bias against finding remittance decay. Second, these studies are generally unable to control for return migration. If individuals who are less successful in the migrant destination are more likely to return, then the only migrants in the sample who have been in the host country for a long period of time are successful migrants who can send large amounts of remittances.

References

Amuedo-Dorantes, Catalina. 2005. "Remittance Patterns of Latin American and Caribbean Immigrants in the United States." Paper presented at the Werner Sichel Lecture-Seminar Series at Western Michigan University in Kalamazoo, MI, October 12.

Central Intelligence Agency (CIA). 2006. *The World Factbook*. Washington, DC: CIA. https://www.cia.gov/cia/publications/factbook/index.html (accessed December 12, 2006).

Connell, John, and Richard P.C. Brown. 2005. "Remittances in the Pacific: An Overview." Asian Development Bank Pacific Studies Series. Manila, Philippines: Asian Development Bank.

Gibson, John, David J. McKenzie, and Halahingano Rohorua. 2006. "How Cost Elastic are Remittances? Estimates from Tongan Migrants in New Zealand." *Pacific Economic Bulletin* 21(1): 112–128.

Global Commission on International Migration (GCIM). 2005. *Migration in an Interconnected World: New Directions for Action*. Report of the Global Commission on International Migration. Geneva: GCIM. http://www.gcim .org/attachements/gcim-complete-report-2005.pdf (accessed September 19, 2006).

Government of Niue. 2004. *Niue Statistics*. Economic Planning, Development and Statistics Unit, Premier's Department. Niue Island: Government of Niue. http://www.spc.int/prism/country/nu/stats/NU_Publications/Population _Estimates/Sept2004HeadCount.pdf (accessed January 3, 2007).

McKenzie, David J., John Gibson, and Steven Stillman. 2006. "How Important is Selection? Experimental vs. Non-experimental Measures of the Income Gains from Migration." World Bank Policy Research Working Paper No. 3906. Washington, DC: World Bank.

Pacific Island–New Zealand Migration Survey (PINZMS). 2007. http://www .pacificmigration.ac.nz.

Parsons, Christopher R., Ronald Skeldon, Terrie L. Walmsley, and L. Alan Winters. 2005. "Quantifying the International Bilateral Movements of Migrants." Working Paper T13. Brighton, UK: World Bank and the Development Research Centre on Migration, Globalisation and Poverty at the University of Sussex.

Puloka, Tevita Tonga Mohenoa. 2003. "Theory and Practice of Misinale in the Free Wesleyan Church of Tonga." Brochure. Nashville, TN: General Board of Discipleship, United Methodist Church. http://www.gbod.org/stewardship/ articles/tonga.pdf (accessed September 19, 2006).

Statistics New Zealand. 2001a. *Niuean People in New Zealand*. Pacific Profiles 2001. Wellington, NZ: Statistics New Zealand. http://www.stats.govt .nz/analytical-reports/pacific-profiles/niuean/default.htm (accessed September 19, 2006).

———. 2001b. *Tokelauan People in New Zealand*. Pacific Profiles 2001. Wellington, NZ: Statistics New Zealand. http://www.stats.govt.nz/ analytical-reports/pacific-profiles/tokelauan/default.htm (accessed September 19, 2006).

Stillman, Steven, David J. McKenzie, and John Gibson. 2006. "Migration and Mental Health: Evidence from a Natural Experiment." BREAD Working Paper No. 123. Cambridge, MA: Bureau for Research in Economic Analysis of Development, Harvard University.

Taumoefolau, Melenaite. 2006. *Tongans: Migrations*. Te Manatu, Tonga: Te Ara, the Encyclopedia of New Zealand. http://www.teara.govt.nz/ NewZealanders/NewZealandPeoples/Tongans/1/en (accessed December 12, 2006).

World Bank. 2005. *Global Economic Prospects 2006: Economic Implications of Remittances and Migration*. Washington, DC: World Bank.

7

The Power of Home

Remittances to Families and Communities

Leah K. VanWey
Indiana University

The past two decades have seen a rapid increase in the value of international migrant remittances; in 2005, their value worldwide conservatively was estimated at $167 billion per year (World Bank 2005). In many cases, these remittances represent a substantial percentage of a migrant-sending country's income and overshadow the official development aid sent from other countries. This has led to research that attempts to determine the effects of remittances on economic development; it has also led to government efforts to encourage the use of remittances for development projects. The body of research is largely inconclusive, as some studies show positive effects and some show that remittances have no effect or negative effects on development. This chapter makes the case that a more complete consideration of the different types of migration around the world, and of the role of social institutions in influencing motivations for remittances, can help us understand these contradictory findings. I develop a typology of migration-remittance systems based on a consideration of social institutions, and I present examples of each type. I conclude with some thoughts about how to construct a theory of the process linking migration and remittances that will predict the future volume of remittances and their effects on economic development.

Past research has focused less on this complete process and more on either the motivations of individual migrants or the uses and effects of remittances. The literature on remittances in the 1970s and 1980s looks at remittances from temporary migrants to their wives, children, and parents in their home communities (Dinerman 1978; Reichert 1981; Rempel and Lobdell 1978; Rubenstein 1992; Weist 1984). The migrants studied were primarily adult male heads of household who had left their fellow household members behind in the home communities. Researchers in this tradition often focused on the ways in which remittances were spent. They argued that migration was motivated by a lack of employment or a low financial return to agriculture in home communities. Migrants left in order to earn money to meet the family's current consumption needs. Therefore, virtually all of the remittances were spent on consumption. These studies are largely pessimistic about the potential for remittances to contribute to the economic development of the home communities. In the words of Joshua Reichert (1981, p. 64), migration "actually serves to maintain (if not increase) the very conditions of underdevelopment, underemployment, and unequal distribution of capital resources that make migration necessary in the first place."

In contrast, the 1990s and early 2000s saw the expansion of a more nuanced approach to remittances, which largely followed the New Economics of Labor Migration (NELM) approach to migration (Stark 1991; Stark and Bloom 1985; Stark and Lucas 1988; Taylor 1992, 1999; Taylor, Rozelle, and de Brauw 2003). NELM sees migration as a response to market failures in developing countries and remittances as part and parcel of the migration process. Migrants leave in large part in order to generate remittances for their home households. The remittances allow the home households to meet consumption needs when other income sources fail, and the remittances also provide them with cash for large purchases. These remittances thus substitute for insurance, smoothing consumption and allowing the home household to undertake riskier agricultural endeavors. They substitute as well for credit markets, allowing the household to make investments that would otherwise be impossible. Researchers in this tradition have, in particular, examined the effects of remittances by considering whole household budgets rather than only considering the way the remittances themselves are spent. Their research shows that remittances loosen household budget constraints, allowing for productive investment as well as increases in consumption (Taylor and Wyatt 1996).

Within this tradition, research has also challenged the pessimistic view of the effects of remittances that are spent on consumption (Durand et al. 1996; Durand, Parrado, and Massey 1996; Massey and Parrado 1994). Migrant-sending households use some of the remittances that are spent on consumption for purchase of local and regional products and services. This spending then drives local and regional economic growth by increasing demand for products and services. Estimates of the multiplier effect of remittances—the amount that the economy grows as a result of each dollar remitted—show the importance of remittances for economic growth in migrant-sending countries (Taylor 1999; Taylor et al. 1996; World Bank 2005). However, the effect of remittances on home communities is less clear, as it depends on how much of the spending of remittances goes for consumer goods from elsewhere in the country or from the migration destinations.

At the same time, other researchers were focusing on individual motivations for remittances, generally within a framework of comparing altruistic motivations to contractual (or exchange) motivations (Agarwal and Horowitz 2002; Hoddinott 1994; Lucas and Stark 1985; Secondi 1997; Stark 1999; Stark and Lucas 1988; VanWey 2004). This research finds that remittance (and migration) patterns vary with the individual characteristics of the migrant. The gender of the migrant, for instance, has important implications for how much and what type of remittance is sent (Curran and Rivero-Fuentes 2003; de la Brière et al. 2002; Osaki 1999; Semyonov and Gorodzeisky 2005; VanWey 2004). The length of migration (Brown 1998) and the age and marital status of the migrant also significantly affect the propensity to remit. While these and other studies take the NELM approach of examining the reasons for the decision to migrate, they also pay attention to the social and cultural context in order to understand who remits, when, and how much. Social networks affect both the pressure to remit and the ability to remit (Roberts and Morris 2003), while social norms influence the expectation by the migrant and the family that a particular type of migrant will remit (Osaki 1999; VanWey 2004). This research also generates debate, in this case about the motivations for remittances. Some studies find support for altruistic motivations, while others find only support for exchange motivations.

Since approximately the turn of the century researchers have been examining a relatively new form of remittance, sometimes called "collective remittances" (Goldring 2004) and sometimes called "social remittances" (Alarcón 2002). These are remittances collected by a group of migrants in a shared destination and returned to their home community for some sort of community project. These projects include social events (such as rodeos and festivals honoring patron saints), infrastructure projects (paving roads, constructing or repairing buildings, installing sewer service), and scholarships for schoolchildren (DeSipio 2002). These have been most extensively studied in modern-day Mexico (Goldring 2004), but this form of remittance is also found in other countries and other eras (Foner 2000; Mohan 2002; Mohan and Zack-Williams 2002).

There are inconsistent findings about the causes and consequences of this form of remittance as well. Cohen (2001) argues that migrants provide these remittances in order to improve their social status in the home community and not out of any altruistic motive. Others contend that migrants are motivated by a concern for the welfare of their home community and by a desire to give back to the community (de la Garza and Lowell 2002). The Mexican government is banking on the second motivation and is encouraging migrants to act on it even more: the government has begun a policy of providing matching funds for remittances sent back for community projects.

Even more vigorously debated is the effect of these projects on community development. Binford (2003) argues that these community projects do not always benefit the whole community, and that often the projects are social in nature and thus have no lasting impact on the community. At the same time, others hold that these projects have positive effects on their own and that they build capacity in the communities. By organizing to complete a project, particularly one that requires interacting with the government to get matching funds, communities develop organizational skills that were not present previously (Díaz-Briquets and Pérez-López 1997; Vertovec 2004).

This chapter seeks to understand the reasons for some of the variation in results researchers have found concerning the motivations of migrants to remit and the effects of remittances on economic development. I argue that social institutions in the home community and the institutionalization of the migration process have important effects on the economic actions of individual migrants. Migration and remittance have traditionally been considered to be individual decisions, motivated by economic concerns. Most simply put, individuals move to places where they expect to make the most money over the long term (Massey and García España 1987; Todaro 1969). Remittances belie the focus on individuals by showing that migration can be a household or a family decision (Stark and Lucas 1988). However, this focus on individuals versus households, with some additional consideration of economic context, has led to contradictory arguments about motivations for remittances, about the levels of remittances to be expected, and about the effects of remittances on development. Given the particular importance of social institutions in influencing gendered family roles and migration (described in the next section), I propose a typology of migration-remittance systems that have distinct underlying rationales and effects on economic development in the home community. In this chapter, I argue that a more careful consideration of the type of migrants coming from a community (a factor that is based in some part on how well developed migration streams are), and of the social institutions in that community, will clarify some of the contradictions.

THE IMPORTANCE OF SOCIAL INSTITUTIONS

All migrants are someone's child, spouse, or parent. The organization of the family and the expectations of individuals filling various roles in the family influence both migration and remittances. The expectations regarding the behavior of individuals in various roles (parent, child, spouse) are also determined by the gender expectations of the community (or country). The combination of gender and family position determines both the ability of an individual to migrate and the expectations of support from any given individual to various others in the family. For example, in many countries social rules indicate that unmarried daughters cannot work (or sometimes even travel) outside the home without supervision by fathers or other male relatives. Often, social rules dictate that one spouse cares for the home while the other provides financial or subsistence support. Similarly, societies vary in the extent to which unmarried children old enough to migrate are expected to contribute domestic work or income to their parents' household. Flows of money and other forms of support from parents to married children or vice versa are also structured by social norms, and strong norms of filial support for aging parents are common in many high-migration societies. Such norms are also gendered: social norms often indicate that support for parents is provided by one particular child (e.g., the youngest daughter, the oldest son) or by one gender of child. Research shows that this often leads to differential investment by parents, as parents give more support to the child who is expected to later support them.

The institutions developed around the migration process itself also have important implications for understanding remittances. As migration becomes more common in a community, the process becomes institutionalized, with widely known procedures and widespread opportunity for migration (Massey 1990; Massey et al. 1994). This leads both to expansion of opportunity to migrate regardless of differences in wealth and education and to more organization of migrants in the destination areas. As the migration stream focuses on one or a few destinations and the population of migrants from a common home community and having common experiences grows, migrants in destinations form organizations based on common home communities (hometown associations). These associations then partially structure the way in which migrants interact with their home communities, affecting the types, amounts, and uses of remittances that they send.

A TYPOLOGY OF MIGRATION-REMITTANCE SYSTEMS

Because of the importance of the roles that migrants or potential migrants play in their families, the typology I propose here focuses in part on the changing types of migrants in terms of their family statuses. The first type of migration-remittance system is a system in which the majority of migrants are male heads of household, the traditional breadwinners in most migrant-sending societies. The second type of system is one in which the majority of migrants are young adults leaving their parents' home to migrate before they have begun to form their own families. The third is a system in which migration is widespread among most types of people in a community. In this type, migration is common enough that hometown associations have formed in the destination, and exchanges of people, ideas, and money between home and destination are common. In this next section, I describe the underlying logic of the migration and remittance decisions for each type and then provide an example of each system from past research.

Migrant Male Heads of Household

The early research on international migrants and their remittances, based largely on international migration from Mexico to the United States, argued that men were leaving their wives and children in their home communities in order to earn money to support them (Dinerman 1978; Massey et al. 1987; Reichert 1981; Weist 1984). These migrants were characterized as target earners who came to the United States to earn money because of a shortage of well-paying jobs in their home communities. Once they earned the target amount—whether it be for consumption for the next year, for a house, or for a piece of land—they returned to their families. The logic underlying this type of migration and remittance is simple: men in migrant-sending regions are unable to earn enough money to start a family (which involves the purchase of materials to build a house and the purchase of a piece of land to begin farming) or to continue supporting their family (either through earning a regular income or by investing in a new business or improvements to their farm).

Migration is an attractive alternative because of the large amounts (relative to the incomes in the home community) that can be earned in relatively short periods of time. Migration becomes most attractive when wages are low or unemployment is high in the home community (Todaro 1969), but it also springs from a failure in certain key economic markets (Stark and Bloom 1985). In particular, most migrant-sending regions have no functional credit or insurance markets. Couples cannot buy a house on credit when they get married; they must have the money in hand. Similarly, new farm machinery or inventory for a new small business must be purchased with cash. Insurance against high health care costs, the failure of crops, and unexpected unemployment is similarly unavailable, making families vulnerable to a dramatic decline in standard of living following these events. To overcome these market failures, to get cash for planned or unplanned expenses, men migrate for short periods to earn specified amounts of money.

The reasoning (based on the migrant's gender-specific role in the family) that motivates these men to both migrate and send (or bring) remittances to their homes is the same reasoning that motivates them to get any sort of job and spend the income on family needs. In Mexico, the majority of migrants have traditionally been men because of norms about appropriate behavior for men and women. Men are expected to support their families by working outside the home and bringing home income. Thus, men not only are expected to earn income, but they have greater freedom of movement outside of the home, making them the clear choice for migration. Following this logic, it is also a foregone conclusion that men will send or bring money home. They migrate solely for the purpose of earning money, and they will be viewed as having failed to support their families if they are not able to send or bring money home.

Massey and colleagues provide clear descriptions of this type of migration from four communities in western Mexico in their book *Return to Aztlán* (Massey et al. 1987) and in later works (Durand, Parrado, and Massey 1996; Massey and Parrado 1994; Parrado 2004). They show that the lifetime probability of migration is very high for men in their study communities, the result of a predictable pattern of migration over the lives of these men. Massey et al. (1987, p. 200) find that "active migration begins at a high level among young unmarried men, falls after marriage, rises with the arrival of children, and then falls again as the children mature and leave home. In short, over the course of a man's life cycle, active migration rises and falls depending on family needs, while the number with migrant experience steadily grows."

The level of migration varies from community to community, depending on economic conditions, but the pattern over the life cycle holds across communities. Parrado (2004) finds that getting the money necessary to set up an independent household is a strong motivator for migration among young men. Massey and Parrado (1994) also find high rates of remitting among migrant household heads (as opposed to unmarried migrants). Using an updated set of survey data covering 22 communities, they estimate that 73 percent of household heads remitted during their last trip to the United States (p. 11), while 58 percent brought money back when they returned (p. 14).

Migrant Children

The second type of migration and remittance in my typology involves the migration of adult children out of their parents' households and their home communities. Like the first type, these moves are often planned as temporary moves, in which children come to work in urban areas or international destinations for a short period of time between stopping school and marrying. Thus the money that they send back is sent to their parents rather than to spouses or children. This type of migration has been extensively studied in Southeast Asia (Elmhirst 2002; Lauby and Stark 1988; Osaki 1999; Trager 1988; VanWey 2004) and in Africa (Hoddinott 1994; Lucas and Stark 1985; Oberai and Singh 1980; Stark and Lucas 1988), and it forms the basis for most of the theorizing about the motivations of individuals to remit.

This type of migration decision follows a different logic from that of the decision of male household heads. Theorists have argued that the decision for these children to migrate is at least partly a household decision, in which parents allocate themselves and their still-dependent children to local or nonlocal employment in order to minimize risk and smooth consumption (Massey et al. 1993; Stark and Lucas 1988). Thus the expectation of remittances on the part of the home household is an integral part of the migration decision. The home households are generally in areas where they face imperfectly functioning or absent markets, leading to a lack of affordable credit and to a lack of insurance against crop failures or price fluctuations. By being employed off farm, migrants provide much-needed cash income for a variety of household purchases. Migration also provides good insurance against income shortfalls because migrants are generally in a geographic region or a sector of the economy providing income that does not covary with the income of the home household. For example, the failure of a rice crop in a migrant-sending region of rural Thailand is generally unrelated to the income earned by a migrant working in construction in Bangkok. If the crop fails or rice prices drop and the home household cannot meet consumption needs, the migrant will still have income that can be used to support the family.

Even though home households send migrants with the expectation of remittances to meet the needs of all household members, the results of empirical studies of this type of migrant show that, at the same time, migrants are self-interested actors (Hoddinott 1994; Lucas and Stark 1985; Stark and Lucas 1988). Migration is important to young adults for improving skills and long-term earning potential, and for meeting new people and seeing new places. It can also be a way for migrants to escape the control of their parents and home communities. Thus the remittances that households receive from these migrants are not completely unselfish. Research shows that home households and migrants engage in informal bargaining, with migrants remitting more to the extent that they expect to benefit more from their relationships with their home households.

The findings on remittances among these young adult migrants closely mirror general studies and theories of intergenerational transfers in the developing world. As in much of the literature on remittances, the intergenerational transfers literature distinguishes between altruistic motivations on the part of children for supporting their parents (considering the parents' needs and sending support in response to those needs) and exchange motivations, in which the transfers between generations are part of a bargain that benefits both children and parents (Frankenberg, Lillard, and Willis 2002; Lee, Parish, and Willis 1994; Lillard and Willis 1997; Quisumbing 1994). The support for altruistic motivations for remittances is relatively weak and shows that the "altruistic" behavior of children is structured by social norms regarding filial responsibility—children that are expected to care for their aging parents are more likely to behave altruistically than are other children. The literature on remittances also shows clear self-interested behavior on the part of migrants who are children of aging parents: they remit more when they expect to return to their home communities (Roberts and Morris 2003; Sana 2005) or when their parents have more land that they may leave to their children in the future (Hoddinott 1994; VanWey 2004).

My work on migrants from villages in rural Thailand provides a good example of this type of remittance (VanWey 2004). This study examines migrants from a sample of villages in Nang Rong district, in the Northeast of Thailand. The majority of the migrants are children leaving their parents' home to migrate to other rural areas, to Bangkok, or to export-oriented manufacturing areas in the Eastern Seaboard of the country. I examine data from a 1994 follow-up survey, in which information was collected from each household about remittances over the previous year from migrants who left the household between an earlier interview (in 1984) and 1994. The relationships between migrants and their home households are characterized by remittances in both directions, but migrants send money or goods home more often than home households send money or goods to migrants. Figure 7.1 shows that home households send some sort of remittance (money or goods) to just under 20 percent of migrants, while more than half of male migrants

Figure 7.1 Migrants and Households Remitting, Nang Rong, Thailand, 1994 (%)

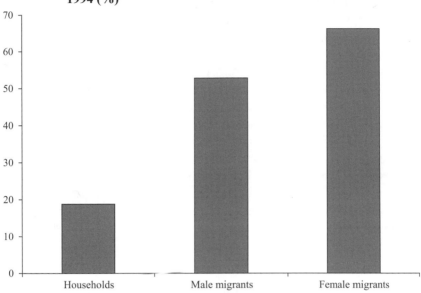

SOURCE· Author's calculations, based on data from the Nang Rong Projects (University of North Carolina 2005).

and two-thirds of female migrants send some sort of remittance to their home households.

From this figure we can see the gender differences in the probability of remitting: women are much more likely to remit. Using multivariate statistical models, I further explored the different determinants of remittances for male and female migrants. I found that both male and female migrants were remitting in ways that suggested self-interested behavior. The more land the home household owned (and therefore could leave to the migrant in the future), the more likely an individual migrant was to send remittances—but only when there were many other migrants from the same household. The migrants were competing with each other for the inheritance. However, female migrants were also acting in a way that suggested altruism, by remitting at higher rates when their parents were in the home household (as they were in most cases). They were substantially more likely to be supporting those parents than were their brothers.

To test whether the differences between male and female migrants in their overall rates of remitting were due to gender differences in things like jobs or wealth of home households, or to differences in how males and females made decisions based on jobs or wealth or the needs of parents, I conducted a simulation analysis. I looked at what would happen if men were like women, both in variables like age, occupation, and education and in the characteristics of the households they left. I then looked at what would happen if each gender had its true values in these characteristics but behaved like the other gender. For example, what if men had the same jobs or education but these characteristics affected them in the way that they affected women? Figure 7.2 shows the results of this analysis. The baseline difference between men and women in remitting (shown in Figure 7.1) is due to differences in how male and female migrants respond to various characteristics, primarily to the presence of their parents in the home household. Even if men were like women in age, education, etc. (bar C), they would not remit

Figure 7.2 Predicted Probability of Male and Female Migrants Remitting, Nang Rong, Thailand, 1994

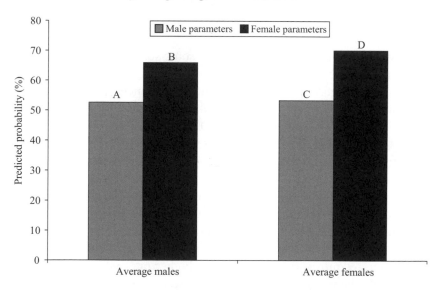

SOURCE: Author's calculations, based on data from the Nang Rong Projects (University of North Carolina 2005).

at the same rate as women. For that result to occur, they would have to behave like women (bar B). Similarly, if women behaved like men (bar C), they would remit less than they actually do (bar D).

These results show that migrants are behaving as we would expect from the literature on intergenerational transfers and relationships. They are bargaining (implicitly) with their parents and siblings for future inheritance of land, and daughters are fulfilling socially expected support roles. In the Thai context, filial support is structured by the tenets of Theravada Buddhism, which say that children must earn religious merit on behalf of their parents to repay the parents for giving them life. Sons are able to do this by spending a short period (about 3 months) becoming ordained monks during early adulthood, while daughters primarily earn religious merit by caring for their families. Thus, daughters who migrate pay this debt through remittances while sons have no such obligation.

Collective Remittances

While some anthropologists and others have noted the importance of associations of migrants in destinations for migrant adaptation to the destination community, and for economic development projects in their home communities (Hirabayashi 1986), widespread study of the remittances from these groups to their home communities has only recently begun (Alarcón 2002). This interest results from the dramatic increase in the value of these remittances as international remittances have grown in volume, and from the Mexican government's attempt to capture some of these remittances for infrastructure projects and other development needs in home communities. Federal, state, and local governments in Mexico now provide matching funds (the amount varies across the country but is usually a 100 or 200 percent match of funds sent by migrant associations). This type of remittance becomes more common as the size of the population of migrants from a given hometown (or home region) in a destination grows. Migrant groups are formed to aid migrants with adaptation and employment in the destination and for social reasons. These groups then collect money to send home to their home communities for parties, infrastructure projects, or other community needs. The extent to which the projects are initiated or controlled by the home communities versus the migrant associations varies from community to community and is itself a function of institutions in the home community, as we will see in the example presented below.

In this setting, the motivations for migration are similar to the previous cases, where migrants leave to earn more money and to overcome the lack of credit and insurance in home communities. However, the longer history and institutionalization of migration has several impacts. The increasing participation of community members in migration leads to migration being a less difficult choice. Migration costs less both financially and psychologically because of three accumulative factors: 1) the ease of finding employment through friends, family, or the hometown association; 2) the familiarity of the people the migrant will find in the destination; and 3) the number of people going back and forth. Migrants now include not only spouses or children but entire nuclear families. The hometown associations and organizations associated with the migration process facilitate the migration and increase the affinity that migrants have for home communities even in the absence of immediate family in the home community.

Remittances then take on a different set of motivations. Collective remittances are fundamentally a social process, as they are collected by an organization in the destination and sent for projects that benefit more than one family in the home community. While migrants still send money to their spouses or parents, they also send money through the hometown associations for the betterment of the home community. The hometown association's stated motivation for this type of remittance is care for the home community and a desire to improve the lives of those remaining there. However, studies also show that the set of social relationships among and between migrant and nonmigrant community members structures remittance behavior. Migrants remit to increase their social status among migrants and nonmigrants alike; indeed, the dense network of social ties between migrants and nonmigrants in this type of migration stream ensures that information is quickly transmitted between these groups. Migrants also remit in order to increase the status and access to resources of their extended family in the home community (Osili 2004), and in order to ensure their continued membership in the community, which is called the option to return (Roberts and Morris 2003).

An example of this type of remittance comes from a study that VanWey, Tucker, and McConnell (2005) completed on remittances to four communities in the central valleys of the state of Oaxaca, Mexico. These communities are unusual for Mexico (though not for Oaxaca) in their system of governance. The four communities are all managed under a system called *usos y costumbres*, by which natural resources are communally owned and all adult male community members have a responsibility for the management of these resources and for the governance of the community. They contribute their labor for the maintenance of communal resources (and community infrastructure) in the form of workdays called *tequio* and must on a regular basis assume positions in community government, called *cargos*, for a few years at a time. These traditional (based on indigenous systems) governance institutions structure the collective remittances received by these communities.

Migrants from these communities are usually men traveling alone or in groups (often leaving their wives and children in the home community) or nuclear families traveling together. Within Mexico, migrants mostly travel to Oaxaca City or to Mexico City; in the United States, they mostly travel to southern California. They migrate largely to obtain better-paying jobs in migration destinations, with the goal of improving their own and their families' standards of living. Virtually all of the migrants remit some money to family members, presumably for the reasons described above (though we did not study this). However, in some of the communities they also send money for missed *tequios*, for community festivals, and for development projects initiated by the origin community.

The primary motivation of these migrants for remitting is a desire to maintain their position and membership in the home community. The obligation to remit is framed as both a moral responsibility and a practical way to avoid adverse consequences for one's remaining family members. As a respondent in Sierra Alta notes, "Supposedly it [paying for missed *tequios*] is voluntary, so it isn't obligatory. More than anything, people here are very conscientious . . . We aren't obligated, but the majority of the migrants would feel bad to come back and not give something . . . So it's really a moral issue."

The home community also uses the threat of restricting access to services or to the benefits of communally owned resources to encourage payment. The president of the Committee on Communal Resources

Table 7.1 Strength of Institutions, Migration, and Remittances for Study Communities, Oaxaca, Mexico, 2002

Community	Strength of institutions	Migration to U.S.	Remittances to community
Sierra Alta	High	Low	High
San Matias	High	High	High
Cerro Verde	Intermediate	Low	Low
San Timoteo	Low	High	Low

SOURCE: Adapted from VanWey, Tucker, and McConnell (2005).

in San Timoteo, one of our study communities, reported, "In the end, what the *municipio* opts to do is to await the moment in which it can lay down the law. That moment comes when someone needs [the services of] the commission. For example, someone says, 'You have to put in a water line.' Well, we're going to do it, but [I reply], 'If you want water, then you owe me five *tequios* that are worth this much, so you have to pay that much.' And that's how we do it."

This motivation explains the variation in the levels of remittance we see sent to the different study communities. Table 7.1 shows the results of our analyses of interview transcripts. The communities that were more strongly organized under the *usos y costumbres* system, with more clearly delineated responsibilities and strictly enforced fines, also received more remittances from migrants. This was unrelated to whether the migrants had gone to other parts of Mexico or to the United States. Thus, stronger community institutions mean that the migrants must remit in order to maintain their community membership and the option of returning to the community.

THE POWER OF HOME AND ITS IMPLICATIONS FOR ECONOMIC DEVELOPMENT

These examples all show the importance of social institutions in the home community and the home country in structuring the decisions of migrants about remittances. That is to say, they all show the power of home over migrants. The rights and responsibilities of men and women, parents and children, determine their opportunities for migration and the amount and reasons they remit. The political institutions in the home community determine the obligations that the migrant has to the home community in order to guarantee the social standing of the remaining family members and his or her own option for return. What initially appears as an economic decision requires a consideration of social institutions.

Given this, migration researchers need to account for these institutions in order to understand empirical results regarding the processes of migration and remittance. Beyond that, we need to theorize on the importance of social institutions. I have provided here a basic typology from my work and that of others, but further theoretical work needs to be done to develop the relationship that exists between migration, remittances, and a variety of social institutions, in order to move beyond an after-the-fact interpretation of results as showing the institutional effects. This theoretical development will also show whether these three categories of migration and remittance systems show the complete variability, or whether additional categories are needed. Furthermore, it will allow us to develop and test hypotheses about the transition from one migration-remittance system to another.

Understanding the effects of institutions and the type of migration will allow us to understand and predict the effects of remittances on economic development. The first type of migration and remittance (migrant male household heads) is essential for the well-being of families in migrant-sending communities. However, it has a debatable impact on economic development in sending communities. Many studies show that the vast majority of the money brought home by these men, or sent home to similar communities, is spent on current expenses or homes (considered consumption expenses rather than productive investments). Yet a review of studies by Taylor (1999) argues that even money spent on consumption will have positive effects on the economy. Remittances spent on consumption free up other resources for productive investment, according to studies of the effects of remittances on all types of spending by households. Additionally, remittances spent on consumption in local communities represent a sizable amount of money and can drive economic growth by increasing demand for locally or regionally produced goods and services (Durand, Parrado, and Massey 1996; Taylor 1999; World Bank 2005).

Remittances that are intergenerational transfers from migrant children to their parents have mixed implications for economic development. They go to parents to support their needs but are likely to come at a time when the parents are not making investments in new land, new technology, or other sorts of capital. The immediate use of these remittances is more likely to be for consumption, but again this might have multiplier effects. Thus, this type of remittance has the potential to bring about economic growth as long as it lasts. The long-term impacts are limited by the lack of productive investment (meaning that the remittances will not have long-term payoffs) and by the time-limited nature of the remittances. Remittances that are used to support parents will obviously not outlast the lives of the parents.

Collective remittances have the most immediate potential for positively affecting economic development. These monies can be used to invest in infrastructure (roads, electricity, schools, sanitation, etc.) that will improve the health and productivity of community residents and potentially allow them to develop or attract businesses. While some past research has suggested that collective remittances do not fund projects desired by the home community (as opposed to projects desired by the migrants), our study shows that home communities can initiate projects and obtain money for them from migrants. In communities such as our study communities, the money can be (and has been) invested in community enterprises that bring additional income and employment to community residents. In this way, remittances might be able to improve home communities to such an extent that future migration would be less desirable.

Further theoretical as well as empirical development of this migration-remittance system typology will allow researchers to predict the future volume and effects of remittances on home communities. If communities move in a rough progression from male heads of household being pioneer migrants to children migrating in a fully developed multilocal social field that includes hometown associations and an institutionalized migration process, we can then predict a progression of effects on local economic development. Initially this progression will be characterized by relatively low levels of remittances (because of the small number of migrants), and these remittances will be used for both consumption and investment by nuclear families who are still rooted in the community. These remittances not only will have multiplier effects because of consumption spending, but they will directly increase productivity by allowing investments of various types. Subsequent to this, remittances to parents will be used primarily for consumption and will only last as long as the parents are living and the children are obligated to support them (for example, they might stop when the children themselves marry or have children). The economic effects of these remittances will occur primarily through consumption spending and multiplier effects. The volume of these remittances may also be higher, given the larger number of migrants participating in the migration stream over time. Finally, the remittances within the fully developed system bypass (or supplement) remittances to families in their economic effects. The fundamental change at this stage in the progression is that the remittances support the production of public goods, which benefits families with and without migrants. This type of remittance has the possibility of eventually evening the standards of living and the life chances of these two groups.

Note

Parts of this chapter are based on empirical work conducted with Catherine Tucker and Eileen McConnell, funded in part by the Center for the Study of Institutions, Population, and Environmental Change and by the College of Arts and Sciences at Indiana University. Other parts are based on dissertation work conducted with support from the Carolina Population Center at the University of North Carolina at Chapel Hill (through a National Institute for Child Health and Human Development training grant). The author also thanks Jorge Chapa, Dennis Conway, Richard Jones, Enrico Marcelli, Una Osili, Susan Pozo, and participants in a miniconference on transnational connectedness at Indiana University, April 2006, for comments on earlier versions of this work.

References

Agarwal, Reena, and Andrew W. Horowitz. 2002. "Are International Remittances Altruism or Insurance? Evidence from Guyana Using Multiple-Migrant Households." *World Development* 30(11): 2033–2044.

Alarcón, Rafael. 2002. "The Development of the Hometown Associations in the United States and the Use of Social Remittances in Mexico." In *Sending Money Home: Hispanic Remittances and Community Development*, Rodolfo O. de la Garza and Briant Lindsay Lowell, eds. Lanham, MD: Rowman and Littlefield, pp. 101–124.

Binford, Leigh. 2003. "Migrant Remittances and (Under)Development in Mexico." *Critique of Anthropology* 23(3): 305–336.

Brown, Richard P.C. 1998. "Do Migrants' Remittances Decline Over Time? Evidence from Tongans and Western Samoans in Australia." *Contemporary Pacific* 10(1): 107–151.

Cohen, Jeffrey H. 2001. "Transnational Migration in Rural Oaxaca, Mexico: Dependency, Development, and the Household." *American Anthropologist* 103(4): 954–967.

Curran, Sara R., and Estela Rivero-Fuentes. 2003. "Engendering Migrant Networks: The Case of Mexican Migration." *Demography* 40(2): 289–307.

de la Brière, Bénédicte, Elisabeth Sadoulet, Alain de Janvry, and Sylvie Lambert. 2002. "The Roles of Destination, Gender, and Household Composition in Explaining Remittances: An Analysis for the Dominican Sierra." *Journal of Development Economics* 68(2): 309–328.

de la Garza, Rodolfo O., and Briant Lindsay Lowell, eds. 2002. *Sending Money Home: Hispanic Remittances and Community Development*. Lanham, MD: Rowman and Littlefield.

DeSipio, Louis. 2002. "Sending Money Home . . . for Now: Remittances and Immigrant Adaptation in the United States." In *Sending Money Home: Hispanic Remittances and Community Development*, Rodolfo O. de la Garza and Briant Lindsay Lowell, eds. Lanham, MD: Rowman and Littlefield, pp. 157–187.

Díaz-Briquets, Sergio, and Jorge Pérez-López. 1997. "Refugee Remittances: Conceptual Issues and the Cuban and Nicaraguan Experiences." *International Migration Review* 31(2): 411–437.

Dinerman, Ina R. 1978. "Patterns of Adaptation among Households of U.S.-Bound Migrants from Michoacán, Mexico." *International Migration Review* 12(4): 485–501.

Durand, Jorge, William Kandel, Emilio A. Parrado, and Douglas S. Massey. 1996. "International Migration and Development in Mexican Communities." *Demography* 33(2): 249–264.

Durand, Jorge, Emilio A. Parrado, and Douglas S. Massey. 1996. "Migradollars and Development: A Reconsideration of the Mexican Case." *International Migration Review* 30(2): 423–444.

Elmhirst, Rebecca. 2002. "Daughters and Displacement: Migration Dynamics in an Indonesian Transmigration Area." *Journal of Development Studies* 38(5): 143–166.

Foner, Nancy. 2000. *From Ellis Island to JFK: New York's Two Great Waves of Immigration*. New Haven: Yale University Press.

Frankenberg, Elizabeth, Lee Lillard, and Robert J. Willis. 2002. "Patterns of

Intergenerational Transfers in Southeast Asia." *Journal of Marriage and Family* 64(3): 627–641.

Goldring, Luin. 2004. "Family and Collective Remittances to Mexico: A Multidimensional Typology." *Development and Change* 35(4): 799–840.

Hirabayashi, Lane Ryo. 1986. "The Migrant Village Association in Latin America: A Comparative Analysis." *Latin American Research Review* 21(3): 7–29.

Hoddinott, John. 1994. "A Model of Migration and Remittances Applied to Western Kenya." *Oxford Economic Papers, New Series* 46(3): 459–476.

Lauby, Jennifer, and Oded Stark. 1988. "Individual Migration as a Family Strategy: Young Women in the Philippines." *Population Studies* 42(3): 473–486.

Lee, Yean-Ju, William L. Parish, and Robert J. Willis. 1994. "Sons, Daughters, and Intergenerational Support in Taiwan." *American Journal of Sociology* 99(4): 1010–1041.

Lillard, Lee A., and Robert J. Willis. 1997. "Motives for Intergenerational Transfers: Evidence from Malaysia." *Demography* 34(1): 115–134.

Lucas, Robert E.B., and Oded Stark. 1985. "Motivations to Remit: Evidence from Botswana." *Journal of Political Economy* 93(5): 901–918.

Massey, Douglas S. 1990. "Social Structure, Household Strategies, and the Cumulative Causation of Migration " *Population Index* 56(1): 3–26.

Massey, Douglas S., Rafael Alarcón, Jorge Durand, and Humberto González. 1987. *Return to Aztlán: The Social Process of International Migration from Western Mexico*. Berkeley and Los Angeles: University of California Press.

Massey, Douglas S., Joaquín Arango, Graeme Hugo, Ali Kouaouci, Adela Pellegrino, and J. Edward Taylor. 1993. "Theories of International Migration: A Review and Appraisal." *Population and Development Review* 19(3): 431–466.

———. 1994. "An Evaluation of International Migration Theory: The North American Case." *Population and Development Review* 20(4): 699–751.

Massey, Douglas S., and Felipe García España. 1987. "The Social Process of International Migration." *Science* 237(4816): 733–738.

Massey, Douglas S., and Emilio Parrado. 1994. "Migradollars: The Remittances and Savings of Mexican Migrants to the USA." *Population Research and Policy Review* 13(1): 3–30.

Mohan, Giles. 2002. "Diaspora and Development: The Black Atlantic and African Transformation." In *Development and Displacement*, Jenny Robinson, ed. Oxford: Open University Press, pp. 77–139.

Mohan, Giles, and Alfred Babatunde Zack-Williams. 2002. "Globalisation from Below: Conceptualising the Role of the African Diasporas in Africa's Development." *Review of African Political Economy* 29(92): 211–236.

Oberai, A.S., and H.K. Manmohan Singh. 1980. "Migration, Remittances, and Rural Development: Findings of a Case Study in the Indian Punjab." *International Labour Review* 119(2): 229–241.

Osaki, Keiko. 1999. "Economic Interactions of Migrants and Their Households of Origin: Are Women More Reliable Supporters?" *Asian and Pacific Migration Journal* 8(4): 447–471.

Osili, Una Okonkwo. 2004. "Migrants and Housing Investments: Theory and Evidence from Nigeria." *Economic Development and Cultural Change* 52(4): 821–849.

Parrado, Emilio A. 2004. "International Migration and Men's Marriage in Western Mexico." *Journal of Comparative Family Studies* 35(1): 51–71.

Quisumbing, Agnes R. 1994. "Intergenerational Transfers in Philippine Rice Villages: Gender Differences in Traditional Inheritance Customs." *Journal of Development Economics* 43(2): 167–195.

Reichert, Joshua S. 1981. "The Migrant Syndrome: Seasonal U.S. Wage Labor and Rural Development in Central Mexico." *Human Organization* 40(1): 56–66.

Rempel, Henry, and Richard A. Lobdell. 1978. "The Role of Urban-to-Rural Remittances in Rural Development." *Journal of Development Studies* 14(3): 324–341.

Roberts, Kenneth D., and Michael D.S. Morris. 2003. "Fortune, Risk, and Remittances: An Application of Option Theory to Participation in Village-Based Migration Networks." *International Migration Review* 37(4): 1252–1281.

Rubenstein, Hymie. 1992. "Migration, Development, and Remittances in Rural Mexico." *International Migration* 30(2): 127–153.

Sana, Mariano. 2005. "Buying Membership in the Transnational Community: Migrant Remittances, Social Status, and Assimilation." *Population Research and Policy Review* 24(3): 231–261.

Secondi, Giorgio. 1997. "Private Monetary Transfers in Rural China: Are Families Altruistic?" *Journal of Development Studies* 33(4): 487–511.

Semyonov, Moshe, and Anastasia Gorodzeisky. 2005. "Labor Migration, Remittances, and Household Income: A Comparison between Filipino and Filipina Overseas Workers." *International Migration Review* 39(1): 45–68.

Stark, Oded. 1991. *The Migration of Labor.* Cambridge, MA: Basil Blackwell.

———. 1999. *Altruism and Beyond: An Economic Analysis of Transfers and Exchanges within Families and Groups.* New York: Cambridge University Press.

Stark, Oded, and David E. Bloom. 1985. "The New Economics of Labor Migration." *American Economic Review* 75(2): 173–178.

Stark, Oded, and Robert E.B. Lucas. 1988. "Migration, Remittances, and the Family." *Economic Development and Cultural Change* 36(3): 465–481.

Taylor, J. Edward. 1992. "Remittances and Inequality Reconsidered: Direct, Indirect, and Intertemporal Effects." *Journal of Policy Modeling* 14(2): 187–208.

———. 1999. "The New Economics of Labour Migration and the Role of Remittances in the Migration Process." *International Migration* 37(1): 63–88.

Taylor, J. Edward, Joaquín Arango, Graeme Hugo, Ali Kouaouci, Douglas S. Massey, and Adela Pellegrino. 1996. "International Migration and National Development." *Population Index* 62(2): 181–212.

Taylor, J. Edward, Scott Rozelle, and Alan de Brauw. 2003. "Migration and Incomes in Source Communities: A New Economics of Migration Perspective from China." *Economic Development and Cultural Change* 52(1): 75–101.

Taylor, J. Edward, and T.J. Wyatt. 1996. "The Shadow Value of Remittances, Income, and Inequality in a Household-Farm Economy." *Journal of Development Studies* 32(6): 899–912.

Todaro, Michael P. 1969. "A Model of Labor Migration and Urban Unemployment in Less Developed Countries." *American Economic Review* 59(1): 138–148.

Trager, Lillian. 1988. *The City Connection: Migration and Family Interdependence in the Philippines*. Ann Arbor, MI: University of Michigan Press.

University of North Carolina. 2005. *Nang Rong Projects*. Carolina Population Center. Chapel Hill, NC: University of North Carolina. http://www.cpc.unc.edu/projects/nangrong (accessed January 2, 2007).

VanWey, Leah K. 2004. "Altruistic and Contractual Remittances between Male and Female Migrants and Households in Rural Thailand." *Demography* 41(4): 739–756.

VanWey, Leah K., Catherine M. Tucker, and Eileen Diaz McConnell. 2005. "Community Organization, Migration, and Remittances in Oaxaca." *Latin American Research Review* 40(1): 83–107.

Vertovec, Steven. 2004. "Trends and Impacts of Migrant Transnationalism." Centre on Migration, Policy and Society Working Paper No. 3. Oxford: University of Oxford.

Weist, Raymond E. 1984. "External Dependency and the Perpetuation of Temporary Migration to the United States." In *Patterns of Undocumented Migration: Mexico and the United States*, Richard C. Jones, ed. Totowa, NJ: Rowman and Allanheld, pp. 110–135.

World Bank. 2005. *Global Economic Prospects 2006: Economic Implications of Remittances and Migration*. Washington, DC: World Bank.

The Authors

Catalina Amuedo-Dorantes is a professor of economics at San Diego State University and is also a research fellow at the Institute for the Study of Labor (IZA) in Bonn, Germany. She is currently on sabbatical and serving as a visiting fellow at the Public Policy Institute of California, where she is working on border enforcement and immigration. Her areas of interest include labor economics, international migration, and international finance, and she has published on contingent work contracts, the informal work sector, immigrant savings, international remittances, and immigrant health care.

C. Simon Fan is an associate professor of economics at Lingnan University, Hong Kong. His primary research areas are development economics, comparative economics, and human capital. His publications have appeared in *Economica, Economic Theory, Economics Letters, Economics of Transition, Journal of Comparative Economics, Journal of Development Economics, Journal of Economic Behavior and Organization, Journal of Population Economics, Kyklos, Labour Economics, Oxford Economic Papers, the Review of Economics and Statistics, Southern Economic Journal*, and other journals and scholarly books.

Robert E.B. Lucas is a professor of economics at Boston University. His research has included work on internal and international migration, employment and human resources, income distribution and intergenerational inequality, international trade and industry, the environment, and sharecropping. He is currently a research affiliate at the MIT Center for International Studies and has served as chief technical adviser to the Malaysia Human Resource Development Program. In 2005, Edward Elgar Press published his book *International Migration and Economic Development: Lessons from Low-Income Countries*.

David J. McKenzie is a senior economist in the Development Research Group at the World Bank. Previously he was an assistant professor of economics at Stanford University. He is co-principal investigator for the Pacific Island-New Zealand Migration Survey and has also published several articles on Mexican migration to the United States. His current research interests include international migration, microenterprises, poverty traps, responses of households to aggregate shocks, and the development of econometric methods useful for working with data from developing countries.

Susan Pozo is a professor of economics at Western Michigan University. She spent the 2006–2007 academic year at the Universidad de Montevideo, Uruguay, as a Fulbright Scholar to measure the impact of remittances on the Uruguayan economy. Her areas of interest include international finance, immigration, and macroeconomics, and her current research focuses on workers' remittances, currency crises, and migration and saving behavior. She is the editor of two previous volumes for the Upjohn Institute, *Essays on Legal and Illegal Immigration* (1986) and *Exploring the Underground Economy: Studies of Illegal and Unreported Activity* (1996).

Oded Stark is a university professor and chair of economic and regional policy at the University of Klagenfurt, a senior fellow at the Center for Development Research, University of Bonn, an honorary university professor of economics at the University of Vienna, a distinguished professor of economics at Warsaw University, a distinguished fellow at the Center of Migration Research, Warsaw University, and research director of ESCE Economic and Social Research Center, Cologne and Eisenstadt. He is the author of *The Migration of Labor* (Blackwell 1991, 1993), and *Altruism and Beyond: An Economic Analysis of Transfers and Exchanges Within Families and Groups* (Cambridge University Press 1995, 1999), and is coeditor of the *Handbook of Population and Family Economics* (in *Handbooks in Economics*; North-Holland 1997). He is a Humboldt Awardee.

Leah K. VanWey is an assistant professor of sociology at Indiana University. She has published papers on migration, remittances, and development in Thailand, Mexico, and Brazil. Her current work integrates sociological and demographic theories of exchange within families.

Christopher Woodruff is an associate professor of economics at the Graduate School of International Relations and Pacific Studies and is director of the Center for U.S.-Mexican Studies at the University of California, San Diego. He has written extensively on small- and medium-sized enterprises in developing and transition economies. His research examines how firms do business with each other in environments in which inadequate legal systems make formal contracting difficult, and the importance of access to finance.

Index

The italic letters *f, n,* and *t* following a page number indicate that the subject information of the heading is within a figure, note, or table, respectively, on that page.

About the Institute

The W.E. Upjohn Institute for Employment Research is a nonprofit research organization devoted to finding and promoting solutions to employment-related problems at the national, state, and local levels. It is an activity of the W.E. Upjohn Unemployment Trustee Corporation, which was established in 1932 to administer a fund set aside by Dr. W.E. Upjohn, founder of the Upjohn Company, to seek ways to counteract the loss of employment income during economic downturns.

The Institute is funded largely by income from the W.E. Upjohn Unemployment Trust, supplemented by outside grants, contracts, and sales of publications. Activities of the Institute comprise the following elements: 1) a research program conducted by a resident staff of professional social scientists; 2) a competitive grant program, which expands and complements the internal research program by providing financial support to researchers outside the Institute; 3) a publications program, which provides the major vehicle for disseminating the research of staff and grantees, as well as other selected works in the field; and 4) an Employment Management Services division, which manages most of the publicly funded employment and training programs in the local area.

The broad objectives of the Institute's research, grant, and publication programs are to 1) promote scholarship and experimentation on issues of public and private employment and unemployment policy, and 2) make knowledge and scholarship relevant and useful to policymakers in their pursuit of solutions to employment and unemployment problems.

Current areas of concentration for these programs include causes, consequences, and measures to alleviate unemployment; social insurance and income maintenance programs; compensation; workforce quality; work arrangements; family labor issues; labor-management relations; and regional economic development and local labor markets.